Lacanian Discourses and the Dramaturgies

Gustavo Geirola

Lacanian Discourses and the Dramaturgies

Translation by Luis L. Esparza

Argus-*a*
Artes & Humanidades
Arts & Humanities

Buenos Aires, Argentina - Los Angeles, EUA
2023

Lacanian Discourses and the Dramaturgies

Spanish title: *Los discursos lacanianos y las dramaturgias*. Argus-*a* Artes y Humanidades/Arts and Humanities, 2022.

Translation by Luis L. Esparza

ISBN 978-1-944508-50-0

Cover illustration: Courtesy of Marco Biachetti in unsplash.
Cover design: Argus-*a*.

Editorial Argus-*a*
1414 Countrywood Ave. # 90
Hacienda Heights, California 91745
U.S.A.
argus.a.org@gmail.com

In memory of Osvaldo Pellettieri

Contents

Foreword

The present book is a revised and enlarged English version of an essay published in Spanish in 2011 in the online journal *Argus-a Artes y Humanidades/Arts & Humanities.*[1]

On that occasion, I decided to dedicate the work to the memory of Osvaldo Pellettieri, who passed away at the very time the essay was being printed. I have decided to keep this dedication because Pellettieri, in spite of our different perspectives on many aspects of theater and theory, was always so kind as to include my writings in the books he published as well as in his journal. He also invited me regularly to the conferences of his GETEA group (Grupo de Estudios de Teatro Argentino e Iberoamericano), to which I managed to attend on some occasions. Now, as then, this book commemorates his name and his work.

While most of the issues of psychoanalysis and theater praxis dealt with in that essay remain untouched, the present book includes excerpts of many other issues that I have developed in detail in later publications. References to these texts, which appeared after 2011 and which deal with the central aspects of theater praxis, can be found in the notes and bibliography. For the last 20 years, I have been trying to conceptualize theater praxis from my own experience as director, and not as researcher.

In 2008, I published an essay on collective creation during the Russian Revolution, which took long hours of reading and research. It appeared in a journal that no longer can be accessed on the web. Since this book deals with collective creation in Latin America, and the essay was central to my own process of reflection on the theatrical, I found it appropriate to include it here in an annex. The essay deals with issues on the field of theater that remain unsolved and which offered me a platform to

[1] Geirola, Gustavo. "Los cuatro discursos lacanianos y las dramaturgias". *Argus-a Artes y Humanidades/Arts & Humanities*, Vol. 1, No. 2, 2011. The original text was revised before being translated into English.

[Translator's note: all quotations in this book have been translated directly from the final Spanish version].

takeoff (in the literal as well as the figurative sense of taking distance) from my own theater praxis.

Readers will surely know how to develop the issues addressed in this book from their own practice, profession and, hopefully, theater praxis, especially if these include psychoanalytic concepts—particularly those from Lacan's work.

Gustavo Geirola
Los Angeles, August 10, 2022

Introduction

In the field of Theater Studies, it is common to distinguish at least four possibilities of work, which we call 'dramaturgies'. They are arranged in a way only apparently diachronic, for they may occur simultaneously:

- The dramaturgy of the author
- The dramaturgy of the director
- Collective creation
- The dramaturgy of the actor[2]

Each one of these possibilities of the theatrical event has its own regulations. The role of the playwright, for example, may exist in any of them but its importance and working style, as well as its power, vary from one to another. The author of the play loses dominion over the spectacle as the play gains autonomy from the text and tries to become a discipline or art form in its own right, independently of literature, where we usually classify plays according to their theatrical genre. However, quite apart from its verbal quality, theater is in all instances a complex art form and

[2] The dramaturgy of the actor is often included in the field of collective creation. However, as we will later see, a departure from this practice is in order here so as to identify the dramaturgy of the actor as is being now developed in Latin America—especially by Eduardo Pavlovsky, Ricardo Bartís, and others. For the purposes of the above list—and to some extent of this work—we think of collective creation in the same way that it is thought of in Latin America: a method that, according to Pavis—not without a few mistakes, as we will later see from the perspective of Enrique Buenaventura—was developed in the 1960s. This method was mostly linked to the experimental and its aim was to overcome the tyranny of the playwright, the text, and the director, who tended to wield power and make all the aesthetic and ideological decisions (*Dictionary of Theatre* 62). Collective creation is then "[a] production not created by a single person (playwright or director) but developed by an entire theater company" (Pavis 62). When stating the difference between collective creation and creative collective, especially after Brecht's mediation, Pavis has no other choice but to propose the idea of the subject *vis-à-vis* the idea of the collective (Pavis 63). As psychoanalysis knows, there may be many individuals (in the theater group, in the audience), but not necessarily many 'subjects'.

as such it defines a poetic that, though not necessarily tied to the word, cannot be independent from the signifier or happen without it. As a place where diverse languages and aesthetic tendencies converge, theater, to be consistent, needs the materiality of the signifier—though not necessarily verbal. Whatever the difficulty encountered in semiotically separating discrete units in non-verbal languages—the failure of theatrical semiotics in this respect being widely known—the truth is that the concept of the signifier, independently of its Saussurean sense, may still be useful to approach theater, not only to analyze the spectacle as a text—as semiotics has unsuccessfully attempted—but to tackle the concrete work of the theater *praxitioner*[3] (be it actor, director, playwright, or all at once) in the specific field of its praxis: the rehearsal. Between the analysis of the dramatic text and the analysis of the spectacle as text there is an unchartered area that has not yet been thought of as a conceptual field in its own right. This area and what goes on within it is the field of work and intervention of what I have called "theater praxis", which cannot be equated to a 'theater institution', that is, a conglomerate of theories, techniques, dramaturgies and, of course, plays. These derive from a long Western theater tradition, particularly from the searing marks left by the *Poetics* of Aristotle and, later, its modern re-elaborations from the sixteenth century onwards.

Quite apart from its possible contributions to the study of the dramatic text and the spectacular text, the Lacanian concept of the signifier, as it unfolds in his early teachings,[4] may open up a series of questions in the field of theater.

[3] The Spanish neologism '*teatrista*' is currently used to refer to those who are capable of performing various roles in a theatrical production, or rotating roles in different productions. In this essay, we have opted for the English neologism *praxitioner* to refer to the theater *practitioner* whose work is based on experience, art craft, and routine, and especially to those whose work is based not on theatrical practice but on *praxis*. Theatrical praxis includes work with performative techniques and routines, with *reality* (both imaginary and symbolic), and the confrontation with the *Real*, in the Lacanian sense of the term.

[4] In this book we shall not deal with the turn that in his *Seminar XX* Lacan makes towards the concept of sign by Charles Sanders Pierce.

In fact, the signifier, as conceptualized by Lacan, is systematically involved with other psychoanalytical concepts—desire, truth, the unconscious, transference, the object *a* and, above all, the subject. This makes it possible to approach a series of questions on *work* and theater production that have not yet been theorized. Though these questions may not be of interest to the traditional student of theater, they are crucial for the theater praxitioner who must deal with the production of the spectacle, a work process that involves many aspects and difficulties often ignored by academics.[5] We must not forget the relationship between art and creativity, the seat of which seems unquestionably to be the unconscious.

Whereas a student of theater can approach the dramatic text as a literary piece that is to a certain extent constant, permanent, and definitive, for the praxitioner it has a truly contingent and temporary existence, for what is written in it may not happen on the stage, and the various circumstances on which its staging depends will inevitably change its meaning, partially or totally. Throughout history, the written testimonies of directors and actors are replete with issues of fidelity and autonomy in relation to the production, *vis-à-vis* the dramatic text. This attests to a usually unresolved conflict over the authorship of the spectacle and the construction of the character. It is in the rehearsal (that crucible of creativity and stage production) where the debate over the sense of the spectacle—and, of course, the critical issue of representation—takes place. Such debate is no other than the discussion, not always aptly posed, over the *truth* of a text.

The crucible of the rehearsal, which begins long before the casting and ends long after the premiere, has not received due attention from theorists, and apart from the experiences of the few praxitioners who have taken to writing them down, no academic texts exist on the subject. Moreover, certain concepts, when passing from the know-how of the praxitioner to the academic discourse of the University undergo changes

[5] See the interviews with Latin American resident directors all over the American continent in the six volumes on *Arte y oficio del director teatral en América Latina* (Art and Craft of the Theater Director in Latin America) that I have published on several occasions. See also the book *¡Todo a pulmón! Entrevistas a diez teatristas argentinos* (At the top of one's lungs! Interviews with Ten Argentinian Theater Praxitioners), co-edited with Lola Proaño.

whose nefarious consequences are evident in many instances on both the concept itself and the theater praxis. For example, the concept of "performance", as developed within a clear-cut frame by a distinguished praxitioner such as Richard Schechner, has been later recycled by Cultural Studies and *applied* to other disciplines after being stripped of its intimate consistency in the work process of the praxitioner and the material conditions of production of a dramatic event. As we shall later see, this kind of sequestration of *savoir*[6] is part of what Lacan calls the Discourse of the Master, except that today it is the university that carries it out. Therefore, the Discourse of the University is complicit with the Discourse of the Master, and eventually with the pseudo-Discourse of Capitalism.

Our interest in this essay is to work from the perspective of the specific needs of the praxitioner at the time of the rehearsal (be it a director, an actor or a playwright) and to tackle the issues at stake (not always with clear rules) in the abovementioned four dramaturgies.

---

[6] Translated into Spanish as *saber*, *savoir* is untranslatable into English. *Savoir* always refers to the unconscious, while knowledge (Fr. *Connaissance*, Sp. *Conocimiento*) is always located in the field of the self and consciousness.

From Saussure to Lacan, from sign to signifier

Lacan takes the signifier beyond the arbitrariness with which Saussure had characterized the sign in his *General Course on Linguistics.* In fact, for Saussure, who distinguishes in French between *langage*, *langue* and *parole*,[7] the signifier does not represent the 'thing' or object but manifests or *expresses* a 'concept', a meaning through a series of organized phonemes—the signifier, according to the rules of the language in which the sign finds its place. For Saussure, the signifier—sound trace[8]—represents the signified as in the famous model in which the word TREE lies on a bar that separates it from the idea of a tree and simultaneously from the sketch of a tree. Both terms (signifier and signified) are encircled together,[9] contained and fused as *sign*, while two inverted arrows try to hold the illusion of a bi-univocal correspondence, as though between them a perfect symmetry existed, as though one reflected the other.

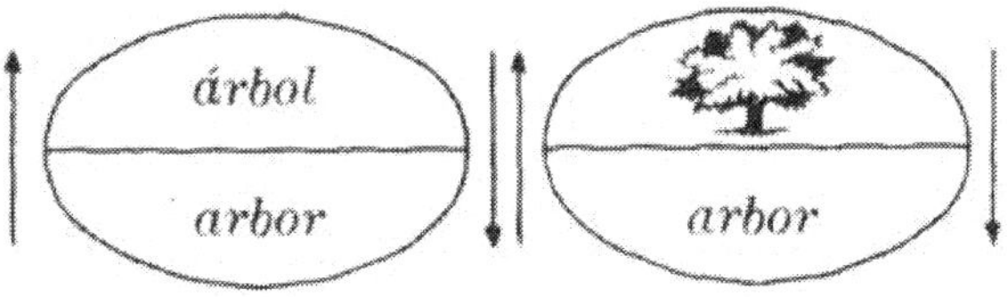

[7] In his *Cours de linguistique générale*, Saussure distinguishes between *langage*, *langue*, and *parole.* These terms have been translated into Spanish as *lenguaje*, *lengua* and *habla.* In English, *langage* has been translated as *speech* or *human speech*; *langue* as *language* and *parole* as *word.*

[8] The idea of 'trace' opens up an interesting door to research in the interstices between linguistics and psychoanalysis, and it is through this avenue that our reconsideration of the topic of memory in our theater praxis should proceed. Freud talked about 'psychic trace' and wrote an excellent essay —"The Mystic Writing Pad" (1924)— which has given way to several interpretations. Lacan would later take several Freudian suggestions, notably from the famous *Letter 52* from Freud to Fliess. In further research projects, it would be interesting to explore the objects *a* (especially the gaze and the voice) in their relation to the drive, the body, and the real, the basis of which is no longer what we know as 'linguistics', but what Lacan christened in his *Seminar 20* as 'linguistery' or 'lingui/steria'.

[9] Saussure uses the money metaphor, talks about "minting" the famous "two sides of the same coin".

Lacan completely transforms this approach to create his famous algorithm S/*s*, in which circles and arrows disappear, the signifier is above the bar—which ceases to presuppose the bi-dimensional and becomes a bar that resists signification—and the signified, as can be seen, is an effect of the signifier. This is why Lacan writes it with a lowercase '*s*', in italics. If the Saussurean model is representational, the Lacanian algorithm is operational in the field of the logic of the signifier.

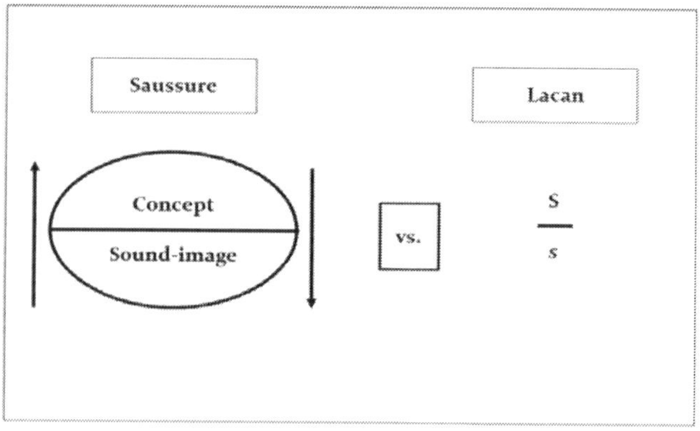

Lacan shows us that language could not be built as an assemblage of *signs* in which signifier and signified come together as a stable unit, for it is precisely in the word, in speech, where a signifier can adopt any meaning. Lacan begins with the premise that signification slides underneath the signifier, that there are no immutable units and that it is precisely the signifying chain that accounts for signification in a retroactive move (that is, from back to front), where the last signifier may change the total meaning of the chain—and, obviously, of all other signifiers. This is why, as we can see in "The instance of the letter in the unconscious or reason since Freud", written after a 1957 talk and included in his *Écrits*, Saussure's model derives into Lacan's S/*s* algorithm. From now on, the signifier will no longer be tied, fixed to a signified, but rather, having ceased to "represent" the signifier as pre-existent—as idealism would have it— it *produces* it according to its place in the signifying chain. Signification is no longer unique; quite the contrary, it becomes ambiguous, equivocal, depending on the chain's process. Lacan goes as far as saying that communication is a misunderstanding, which puts into question the Jakobsonian model of language functions in which an addresser sends a message to an addressee and, if they share the same code and there is no interference, the message's meaning can be shared by both. But for Lacan misunderstanding is something else than just the upsetting of meaning, something beyond the difference between hearing and listening. In Lacan the signifying chain is formed by rings that open up to other rings ("rings in a chain bound to another chain of rings" [*Écrits I* 496]. But the linearity of this must not mislead us into thinking that meaning derives from the aggregation of signifiers, as in a sum total. Nor should we think of this as an effect or result of such linearity. We must not forget that a discourse—that dimension contained in the Other, beyond speech, the word, and exceeding it—includes a polyphony, which emerges as a score made of several musical staffs, as demonstrated by the Saussurean concept of the anagram (closer to the letter, to writing and, obviously, not corresponding to the perspective institutionalized by the *Course on General Linguistics*). This allows Lacan to think of the signifying chain as something that says more than is intended and even says a different thing (*Écrits I* 470).

What Lacan keeps from Saussure is the idea of difference. As in the phonologic system, a signifier differs from another in some of its traits. Known as the diacritic principle, this means that a phoneme is what others are not. Lacan also introduces the idea that meaning is produced retroactively, for the addition of a new signifier may change the signification of all the preceding ones and of the chain itself. Even in its repetition, a signifier is always another, so no stable identity can be attributed to it. Not even in a tautology such as "life is life", or "I am I", can we assume that the first signifier and its predicate are the same. Similarly, in the phrase "my *mise-en-scène* is my *mise-en-scène*" often heard among certain praxitioners, there is no place for a tautology, for no staging is ever the same. Language appears as a network of multiple remissions from one signifier to another and the meaning in the chain does not reside in any of the signifiers involved, their signification being to a certain extent suspended, dependent on their place in the chain and their contextual relations with one another: "it can be said that it is in the signifying chain where the meaning *insists*, but none of them *consists* in the signification of which it is capable of at the very moment" (*Écrits I* 470). However, in doing a case-by-case analysis of signifiers in an utterance, we must remember to pay attention to the symbolic registry of language, the famous Other (with a capital O) as the signifiers' treasure, as the code against which their difference in meaning can be measured.

Underlying many statements by praxitioners is the idea that the subject's mind is the seat of meaning and that the signifier simply provides the material support for its expression. But meaning, says Lacan, does not predate the signifier and cannot exist without it. Even the most sagacious of praxitioners seem to cling to this problematic and deep-rooted residue of idealism, which takes them to many blind alleys in their reflections, often with dire consequences. For many of these praxitioners, a spectacle stems from an idea (a dramatic text, a topic, etc.), a piece of supposed knowledge that the play is going to 'represent'. This is the typical model of the theater institution. But theater praxis, as we will see, stems from the unknown *savoir* of the unconscious and stages a *mise-en-scène* of multiple meanings, which, at the most, outlines an idea or several ideas from images that are enigmatic or cyphered, not necessarily cryptic. If there is a meaning, a 'truth', it is because it emerges from the play of signifiers, and the subject is precisely an effect of the signifier. There is a subject only when the word is articulated and this subject (who is not an individual) not necessarily knows what he[10] is saying. The subject comes up, precisely, as a vacuum between two signifiers, $S_1 \rightarrow S_2$. It is neither an individual, nor a person. The combination of signifiers (metonymy) and their substitution (metaphor) allow us to capture the way in which the utterance promotes the subject. It would suffice to refer to the example of the linguistic lapse in order to realize that the moment the speaker wants to say something somebody speaks for him and, to his surprise, says an unexpected thing: where there should be a signifier, an unexpected one appears in its

[10] Throughout this book, we shall keep masculine pronouns (he, his, him) as they appear in the original texts, in the understanding that they refer not to persons with a defined gender but to categories. An alternative to this would probably be the use of the neutral 'it', but that would create unnecessary confusion for the reader.

stead, catching the speaker unawares and, in this way, we can see to what extent the subject, more than speaking—in the sense of the active voice—is spoken by the Other. Consciousness then cannot be conceived of as possessing its own meaning, for it is superseded by the unconscious. For all its artistic achievements, the theatrical endeavor is but a routine in the theater institution. When it explores creativity in the dimension of the unconscious, theater praxis is oriented elsewhere, to a place where applying formulae or concepts is impossible, not even those of psychoanalysis.

Consequently, every utterance is to a certain extent ciphered for the speaker, who turns into a divided subject—described by Lacan as $ [a barred S]—and the truth of what is being said is an effect of the word as it is captured by another speaker. The word of the *analysand*, his speech, his 'concrete discourse' is psychoanalysis' medium (*Écrits I* 240), a word that "calls for an answer" (*Écrits I* 241) and is directed to a listener even if he does not respond, even if the *analysand* finds nothing but silence. It is through this word, directed to another, that the subject assumes his story, which takes us back to the divided subject who does not know everything he says and cannot remember all his past.[11] 'Truth' is precisely that which is repressed, so unbearable that the subject chooses to know nothing about it. Truth settles then at the level of that lack, of that hole, which, in any case, insists on affecting the continuity of the signifying chain through ruptures, fractures, suspensions, blunders, and silences. Unaware of himself and his truth, the 'I' of consciousness struggles to act as the master of meaning, as though he knew all he says. And with this collapses also the idea of the referential illusion, namely, that the discourse is somehow shaped according to things, to reality. This illusion of knowing, of authorship, is now relativized, dependent on the reception of meaning in an inverted way—that is, on listening to the other/Other. This is why Lacan

[11] This is what praxitioners (and even researchers!) mean when they resort to the popular phrase "it is up to the audience to complete the meaning of the show", a statement that is only partially correct from the perspective of Lacanian theater praxis. To complete is not to supplement. The space that separates the stage from the audience — which can be thought of as a littoral, a concept used by Lacan— must be subject to concrete analysis, especially from the perspective of Lacan's formulae of sexuation.

limits the referentiality between signifiers by affirming that a signifier is what a subject represents for another signifier. The Lacanian subject is not an organism, nor does he correspond to the psychological self. Rather, he is the result of the signification game. Lacan liked to say that the subject is in permanent interdict (*interdit*),[12] located in that elusive space opened by the signifiers and without being able to be any of them. One way to represent this numerically is by means of the formula $S_1 \rightarrow S_2$, an operation that, as we will see, produces an irretrievable residue, which Lacan will designate as object *a* to indicate that prohibited, inaccessible, unnameable *jouissance*.

Language, or the symbolic register, which Lacan writes as A (*Autre* = 'Other') and precedes the entry of the individual into it, awaits him and even survives him—in the form of the proper name or paternal surname in our culture—cannot cover all that is Real, for it is as though it were detached from things. If there is a reference for a signifier, it is just another signifier. Thus, we have a conceptual difference between 'reality' (a word always on the lips of playwrights) and the Real. Reality is a discursive, phantasmal construction of the self as a defense against the Real, those discontents in civilization that the self cannot completely dress, cover with images, verbalize; that Real, that *jouissance* caused, however, by the deadly inscription of the signifier and the Other in order to capture the human offspring as a member of society. The Real is what remains of the subject's renunciation to satisfactions not allowed by the Other and finds itself at the base of repetition, from where the subject always wants but fails to retrieve it. Lacan refers to the 'discourse of the Other' to indicate the reservoir of signifiers and combinations—already more or less stabilized—that precede the individual's entrance; the Other, as language, has thus a trans-individual dimension, a term that Lacan will also use to refer to the unconscious, avoiding the use of the word "collective", which presupposes the sign and not the signifier. The sign represents something to someone, whereas the signifier represents a subject for another signifier. Hence, the collective unconscious, for example in Jung, seems to be more

[12] The French *interdit* alludes to what is 'in between', what is said and what is forbidden.

affiliated with the Saussurean concept of language and sign, as stable and univocal entities, and consequently has nothing to do with the Freudian-Lacanian approach based on the signifier.[13] The Lacanian perspective of the signifier and the unconscious could not admit the adjective "collective", because for Lacan the unconscious (even language) is 'parochial', that is, nothing universal or essential or hidden or latent, or ahistorical, but just the opposite: it is the unconscious of a group or a community in the here-and-now of its existence. Each theater group has 'its' unconscious, for which there is no dictionary of symbols to help.

Lacan will also bar the Other (Ⱥ), because there is also a lack in him and, in subsequent elaborations, he will be linked to the object *a* and to the register of the Real. This Other also lacks a signifier that could decide the meaning of all the others—as in a theological approach—and grant a definitive meaning to each signifier, the 'guarantees' that the Other would be bound to provide and, obviously, never provides. All this leads Lacan to say that "there is no metalanguage", that is, there is no language that fixes the meaning of another previous language. What there is in the Other is a missing signifier, which is precisely what allows the constant movement of all signifiers, the continuous ambiguity, the incessant sliding of meaning underneath the signifier. And the phallus must also be mentioned, not as an organ or a privilege of the masculine over the feminine, but as "the signifier of the lack in the Other", that lack in the symbolic without which the subject could not come about. Such lack indicates that there is a 'desire of the Other', which causes the desire of the subject, a lack in the subject.[14]

[13] Psychoanalysts have abundantly discussed the issue of the signifier in Freud's work and some have tried to refute Lacan; however, it would suffice to approach three major works by Freud: *The interpretation of dreams, Psychopathology of everyday life* or *Jokes and their Relation to the Unconscious*, to realize the relevance of the signifier in Freudian psychoanalysis.

[14] The issue of the phallus as a privileged signifier in the symbolic register (conceived of as a battery of signifiers) has raised enormous controversy. How would the phallus as signifier be different from other signifiers? This is not the place to elaborate on this issue.

This seemingly anti-theological approach is also a way of positing the impossibility of fixing the meaning of each signifier, that is, the cancellation of any claim to power over the signifiers in order to make them signify uniquely and universally. However, the symbolic register, the Other, has, on the other hand, a certain stability, dictionaries that must be reviewed with certain periodicity, which is what consequently allows us to measure the variation, the deviation, the misunderstanding produced by the imaginary. Partly following Saussure, Lacan conceives of the Other as a treasure, unstable and open.

The subject of psychoanalysis is divided, and the bar that Lacan puts on the S (*$*) to represent symbolic castration is what allows him to pose the question of desire. Although we shall not dwell now on the long Lacanian elaboration of the object *a* (first as an object, as the goal of desire, and later as the cause of desire and *jouissance* and surplus-*jouissance*), nor to detail Lacan's proposals about the mirror stage and the model of the inverted vase and then the corsage,[15] we are nevertheless going to insist on how the bar is what prevents the subject from reaching the object of his desire, his truth. Desire is always desire for an object lost forever; desire is always a lack, a lack that cannot be filled. The subject manages, however, to give himself some kind of temporary satisfaction resorting to substitute objects for the lost object; it is a metaphoric-metonymical operation through which desire slides without reaching its satisfaction or full *jouissance*. There is, then, something lost forever, because the signifier cannot represent the subject in its entirety, there is always a loss, a lack-in-being represented in the Lacanian algebra as object *a*. The a*utre* object or the other as object is identified as the goal of desire in the first Lacanian seminar and then as the cause of desire, especially from *Seminar 10, Anguish*. Desire is always desire to retrieve the missing part; the object *a* will be

[15] For the relationships between these Lacanian concepts and theater praxis, see my "Aproximación lacaniana a la teatralidad del teatro: desde la fase del espejo al modelo óptico. Notas para interrogar nuestras ideas cotidianas sobre el teatro y el realismo" (Lacanian approach to theater's theatricality: from the mirror phase to the optical model. Notes to interrogate our everyday ideas about theater and realism). I have recently published a long essay under the title "Interpretando el adjetivo 'áfono' en relación a la voz como objeto a" (Interpreting the adjective 'aphone' in relation to the voice as object *a*), where I elaborate more specifically on these issues.

later conceived of by Lacan as an organ, as detachable parts of the body that cannot be reassembled (the bosom, the feces, the gaze, the voice), and this will take Lacan to make complex elaborations on the anal, the scopic and the invoking drives. The *fantasme*, represented by the formula *$◊a*, will function as a screen that regulates the subject's access to object *a*, to *jouissance*, and to some extent rescues the subject from the alienation of the *jouissance* of the Other that could make him disappear, drawn him into *jouissance*, lead him to death.

What is a discourse?

Far from even attempting to encompass the meticulous and exhaustive work of Lacan, this succinct introduction to its central ideas furnishes us with some tools to understand the contribution of the four discourses to the study of dramaturgy.[16] Lacan understands discourse as "a necessary structure that exceeds by far the word, a more or less occasional occurrence" (*Seminar 17* 10), and which "can subsist without it" (*Seminar 17* 10). The Lacanian discourse is what binds society together, and each discourse establishes an exercise of power, knowledge, and *jouissance* of some kind. For example, an Italian-style theater hall has a theatrical discourse already embedded in it that precedes the play and imposes a certain politics of gaze (Geirola "Aproximación"). The same happens to the spatial arrangement in a learning institution: a traditional classroom has a desk with a blackboard behind it, facing a certain number of tables and chairs. There is silence; nobody talks, for the Other has installed therein an educational discourse. In that given *place*, with a series of windows, doors, four walls, and given measures, several *spaces*[17] can be built, and each one of them will respond to a different type of discourse. Though obviously

[16] We shall later refer to a pseudo-discourse, a modality or style of the discourse of the Master, which Lacan incorporates in 1972 and names the Capitalist discourse".

[17] Theater praxitioners often create confusion when they use "place" and "space" as ideological notions, in an ordinary sense, rather than with their precise meaning. See on this problem my book *Sueño. Improvisación. Teatro. Ensayos sobre la praxis teatral* (Dream. Improvisation. Theater. Essays on Theater Praxis).

responding to a given architectural discourse, the place remains physically unchanged while the space—that is, the discursive relations of knowledge/power—is constructed, its consistency being ultimately political and, therefore, subvertible. Many spaces (thought of as relations) can be built, produced in the same place.[18] As we shall see in the four Lacanian discourses, the discourse designs specific positions for the transmission of *savoir* and knowledge, as well as strategies to (not) deal with *savoir* and truth. Back to the example of the classroom, we can say that the so-called "students" come in and go directly to sit on the chairs, while someone enters and stands between the desk and the blackboard. This individual has not said a word yet, but the students are already taking notes. What the "teacher" says is taken as "true". The institution attributes that role to anyone occupying that specific site, and guarantees it in the institution's hiring protocols. The person could well be a runaway from a psychiatric institution who had the occurrence of entering the classroom and sitting at the desk and start saying something. What would happen if it were one of the students? The discourse is already there, even before a word has been said. Participants in a theater acting techniques workshop hardly ever discuss these questions: what silent discourse is there before the beginning of the rehearsal, the act or the play? Would other politics of gaze bring other meanings to the scene? What would happen if a spectator were to sit on the stage or any other "unexpected" site? Theatricality is *naturally* assumed as a determination with no political impact, as though the political were "expressed" onstage only in the play's contents and theatricality were a fatality, the only way of seeing and being seen. Theater practitioners are so obsessed with the play, with its subject matter, with the originality of the staging, that they forget that, no matter what they do, unless

[18] This brings us to the question—which we will not be able to tackle in this essay—of the Freudian structures of neurosis, perversion, and psychosis in theater praxis, which in a staging directed at a subject (the spectator) work for Lacan as masks constructed by the project or discursive design and are not to be confused with the individual and the people that finally come to see the performance. See my essays "El director y su público: la puesta en escena y las estructuras espectatoriales" (The director and his audience: the staging and the spectacle-pertaining structures) and "Praxis teatral y puesta en escena: la psicosis como máscara espectatorial en el ensayo teatral" (Theater practice and staging: psychosis as a spectator's mask in the theater rehearsal), parts One and Two.

they work with theatricality and the politics of gaze, the work is bound to miss its intended effect. Even those theater proposals whose meaning or purpose go against the perverse protocols of the theater institution (some even calling for emancipation) end up being trapped in the violence established by the discourse of the theatricality of theater: a silent audience sitting in an immovable seat in a dark space, ready to enjoy the role of the voyeur. Theater practitioners seldom wonder about which discursive strategy would be more adequate to say what they or the text want to say. I have tried to develop this idea from a theater-logic perspective in my book *Teatralidad y experiencia política en América Latina* (Theatricality and Political Experience in Latin America), in which I identify at least six theatrical structures, one of them being the theatricality of theater. This bourgeois, modern theatricality has managed to establish and naturalize itself as hegemonic discourse. Theater praxitioners fail to ask themselves whether the spatial design of the theatricality involved coincides or clashes with what they intend to say in aesthetic and political terms. Justifications to comply with the theatricality of theater abound: financial, moral, personal, institutional, etc., but they can never justify the obedience from an artistic and critical viewpoint. Built during the European Renaissance as a white, aristocratic and later bourgeois institution, in total consonance with Capitalism and Western modernity, the theatricality of theater (manifest in the Italian-style theater hall and its variations, even when it is reproduced in the street!) is in charge of suffocating (and sometimes annulling) the most daring transgressions on the stage. The theatricality of theater could well be part of what Lacan would call, at the end of his teachings, the crazy cunning of Capitalist discourse, which, as such, is doomed to blow up.

Some eloquent examples of theatricality and discourses

I have played with these issues in my courses and workshops. On one occasion, during a seminar for teachers at the University of Salta, I had two desks (with a water jar and a glass, as good manners dictate) placed on opposite sides of an empty classroom, and a blackboard behind each of them. The chairs had been stacked up against one wall. It was a mirror disposition. Looking from where nobody could recognize me as the instructor, I observed the attendants' amazement when they didn't know where to go for a seat. When I came in and reached one of the chairs, the participants immediately sat in front of me; some resisted for a while until their pain in the neck finally made them turn and comply with the power of the Master. I often make this kind of spectacles in which the *natural* protocols of the theatricality of theater are suspended: without chairs, without stage, attendants do not know where they are expected to place themselves as spectators (nobody is a spectator before entering the theatrical discourse, regardless of its structure), they do not know where the staging space will be and thus face the un-naturalness of theatricality. On another occasion, I staged a spectacle at the Arizona State University entitled *What is love?* It consisted of three brief pieces, one by a Spanish dramaturge and the other two by Latin American dramaturges, all women. More than their contents, all related to love, what mattered to me was the theatrical discourse in which I wanted them to play: there were bleachers of three or four levels, very long and high, on which chairs were placed. The attendants, all university people, most of them postgraduate students, came in and found a place. The lights were turned off and as the show was about to begin, spectators found out that the action didn't take place *before* the audience (as was expected to *naturally* happen) but to one side. Disguised as a spectator, one actor moved his chair and repositioned it in the direction of the scene, so as to watch more comfortably. As the show began, in a gesture that made the audience see to what extent theatricality is a convention, a contract, a discourse with nothing natural about it, one of the actresses, visibly annoyed, asked for the lights to be turned on, interrupted the show, and ordered the spectator to return his seat to its original place, which he did reluctantly. As a director, I always like to state the rules of the game from the beginning. The opening ritual is resumed, lights go off and after a few minutes, the spectator moves again his chair and places it in a more comfortable position. He takes out a flashlight and begins to check the lines as the actresses say them. The discourse of love is always a varied repetition, a combination of figures, as Roland Barthes taught us in his *Fragments of a lover's discourse*. The audience, a bit confused, looked sideways at the stage, with their heads placed at an angle towards the right side, trying to comply with the perverse convention in silence. The actor-spectator went on, asking at times for a change of tone from the actresses, for something more or less melodramatic, according to what he thought were the right codes to talk about love. The second play demanded a sharper turn of neck from the audience, since it took place further to the right side and people sitting on the bleachers had to stick out their necks to be able to see. Finally, the last play was performed towards the back of the bleachers, which made it virtually impossible for the audience to see unless they got up from their chairs or moved them, which nobody did. At the end of the show, a spectator who knew me came to complain, in a rather incensed tone, that she had been unable to see a thing. I watched her surprised, because she happened to be one of the doctoral candidates with a well-known radical feminist position, and I replied: How do you intend to change women's situation when you're not even capable of moving a chair and defend your right to see?

Let's see another example. On the occasion of my doctoral exam in the same university, in which I didn't know from what and from whom I had to 'defend' my thesis—a ritual that to me had a medieval, feudal taste, anchored in an academic discourse of the late twentieth century—it occurred to me to performatively convey what I had written in theoretical terms. The jury had already installed themselves beside a desk reserved for me, with chairs in front for whomever came to accompany me in such a meaningful academic event. I had previously requested a video player and a TV set to show a video, which had not elicited any suspicion, since the dissertation was about Latin American theater. Upon entering, I went to sit among the audience. I had with me a written text to present my dissertation, which I passed on to a classmate to read out loud. As soon as the jury declared the ceremony formally open, she began to read from her seat, which created major disagreement and somebody interrupted. I made my point saying that I was the author of the text, but evidently, I was told, it had to be pronounced by me. I then stood up, turned on the recorder and went back to my seat among the audience. The magnetic tape began to play my voice reading the same text. But this wasn't enough. I was told that I had to read it out loud and I began to do so from the seat I had taken, which made many to turn to see me. Someone complained again and then I was asked to occupy a frontal position and read before the audience, who wanted to see me. Then, not moving from my seat yet, I turned on the video, where I appeared reading the same text, which still wasn't enough. They wanted my body to occupy the desk and read my text. This was more important than the quality of my dissertation or the potency of my ideas. Sitting at the site in which the discourse of the university expected me to sit was obviously a long-established convention that my doctoral candidacy could not challenge. It came as a surprise to me to see that academia so diligently discussed the need to use more technology in teaching, on the one hand, while on the other it was so obstinate in keeping the feudal-juridical rituals of the transmission of knowledge. After all, I could have made my 'defense' from anywhere in the world if the interest had really been on what I had to say. But, as this case of theatricality in action demonstrates, this was not the case.

Finally, I would like to mention a recent book, *Espacio escénico. Texto, contexto y sentido* (The Space of the Stage. Text, Context, and Meaning) by architect and stage designer Juan Carlos Malcún, who accompanied me in a staging of Emilio Carballido's *Yo también hablo de la rosa* at the University of Tucuman, which I have described elsewhere. The book analyzes three different projects by different theater groups of Carlos Gorostiza's *Los prójimos* (The next others) staged on different days. Each one of them responds to variations in the dramatic text but also to changes in meaning coming from spatial devices, which, as we have seen, are also a type of discourse. Malcún's book includes one chapter on the design for a staging of a play presented by Mauricio Rosencof in Tucuman. The conflict between director and stage designer in this chapter shows the tensions between the theater institution and its system of production: a conventional project by a director who didn't understand the stage designer's proposal and, in a rather subservient position to the State, insists on keeping the curtain when, precisely, the staging proposal aimed at a direction opposed to the theatricality of theater, a staggering example of a misunderstanding between these two theater practitioners.

Lacan's four discourses

In the foregoing section, we have gradually introduced the four algebraic symbols used by Lacan to present his four discourses in *Seminar 17 The Other Side of Psychoanalysis* (and its supplement *Radiophone*) and in *Seminar 20 Encore*. Lacan conceives of S_1, S_2, barred S ($) and object *a* as the four articulation possibilities acquired by the symbolic as a social bond based on language. The social bond is designated then as a discourse (*Seminar 20* 68). We then have:

S_1: the Master signifier
S_2: *savoir*
$ (barred S): the subject
a: surplus *jouissance*

The rotation of these four discourses —"four structures" (*Seminar 17* 12) or "gyrating four-legged devices" (*Seminar 17* 15)— through each of the four places (the Agent or the place of semblance[19], the Other, Truth, and Production) are called the discourse of the Master, the discourse of the University, the discourse of the Hysteric (sometimes wrongly called "of hysteria")[20] and the discourse of the Analyst. The places are laid out as follows:

$$\frac{\text{Agent}}{\text{Truth}} \rightarrow \frac{\text{Other}}{\text{Production}}$$

[19] *Semblant.* Lacan uses this term to refer to an appearance in psychoanalysis, which differs from the appearance in science, for which he uses *apparence*. See Evans, Dylan. *An Introductory Dictionary of Lacanian Psychoanalysis*, Routledge, London/New York, 2006, p. 178 [Translator's Note].

[20] As a way to pay homage to hysterical women, the touchstone of psychoanalysis, Lacan calls this not "the discourse of hysteria", as has sometimes been translated, but "the Discourse of the Hysteric", which must always be read as a female hysteric.

The use of the arrow (→) appears in *Radiophone* and in *Seminar 20* as the impossibility of the discourse of the Master and the discourse of the Analyst; but in the same texts Lacan uses it in the inverted sense (‹) to refer to impotence in the discourses of the University and of the Hysteric. However, we shall keep two bars (//) here to refer to the disjunction between truth—always the foundation of what is said, and which is always hidden from the Agent, beyond his unconscious intentions—and production, for what is discursively articulated is not linked to truth. The Agent, however, is not that who does, "but that who is made to act" (*Seminar 17* 182) insofar as he responds to the demand of the Other and this, in Lacanian terms, means that "it is not sufficiently clear whether the Master will work" (*Seminar 17* 182), that is, that he will act autonomously, as an engine or as an original impulse. The Master functions always on behalf of the Other, on demand by the Other. As we have shown, these discourses are, in a way, *already there*; we do not choose them, rather, they model our saying and doing, take us beyond the place we would like to reach voluntarily, "beyond effective enunciations" (*Seminar 17* 11), with consequences we cannot foresee or control.

S_1, the Master signifier, represents the subject and does it (imaginarily, illusorily) as whole, concealing his castration, which nonetheless makes itself explicit in $\$$, the divided subject (consciously and unconsciously), the desiring subject who ignores the cause of his desire.[21] S_2 is *savoir*, that is, the network of signifiers minus S_1, which, as the field of language, is both conscious and unconscious. In the discourse of the Master, Lacan differentiates between the *savoir* of the Slave[22] and the *savoir* of the old Master,

[21] For the reader unfamiliar with psychoanalysis, it is important to note that 'castration' does not mean 'emasculation'. The concept of castration refers to the fact that, in order for the human offspring to become a human subject that is part of a social bond, he must give up the satisfaction of drives such as incest, parricide, aggressiveness, etc. The subject is thus divided and registers a lack. We must remember that neither the symbolic Other is complete: it is not A, but barred A (Ⱥ)—that is, he also registers castration.

[22] Lacan points out that in Hegel Master and Slave are of the same sex, and for this reason, the relationship is about "knowing what is that which the Master receives, under the name of this surplus *jouissance*, from the work of the Slave" (*Seminar* 17 189). If they were man and woman, the question of *jouissance* would be a "truly sublime" one (*Seminar* 17 189). The male slave, who at first does not want to give up *jouissance*, finally does so

and more recently, as in the case of the University, between the *savoir* of the modern Master and the *savoir* of S_2. The Slave, as we shall see, "knows how to do" his work, he is "the one who constitutes an unrevealed unconscious" (*Seminar 17* 30) inasmuch as he imperceptibly produces *a* as surplus value. The Master does not want to know anything at all; he just wants to enjoy what derives from the work of the other, the Slave. But Lacan emphasizes something we shall return to later on, namely that "what leads to *savoir* is not the desire to know. What leads to *savoir* is... the discourse of the hysteric" (*Seminar 17* 22). This is why, in his *Television* (1973) he begins to homologate science to the discourse of the Hysteric, whereas in his early seminars the homologation was with the discourse of the Master. Lacan differentiates in this way the discourse of science from the discourse of the University, the latter conceived of as totalizing, encyclopedic, academic. The *savoir* to which Lacan refers and is of interest to psychoanalysis, is one that, as opposed to knowledge and representation, is unknown (*Seminar 17* 30). As does the hysteric, science relates to the real, the dysfunctional, which escapes totalization. Never content with closed systems, science always interrogates them. Finally, we have object *a*, which, having fallen from S_2 on the latter's entry in the symbolic order, escapes the network of signifiers and represents the expelled, the abject, a cause rather than the aim of desire. This irretrievable object constitutes the subject's lack-in-being, that is, something he misses in order to have access to *jouissance* as an absolute, full satisfaction, and therefore he will have to make do with a surplus *jouissance*—which, in reality, is a minus *jouissance*. The subject is then thrown into a chain of substitute objects that will never attain *a*. It is this unsatisfiable object what drives the subject to transcend his limits in search for an impossible satisfaction that, to a certain extent, is also fatal. As Lacan states in his earlier teachings, object *a* works simultaneously as the cause of desire and the goal of desire—it works backwards and forwards. Illusorily, the subject believes that the

and "substitutes it for work, which is certainly not its equivalent" (*Seminar* 17 184). This opens up multiple questions in relation to theatrical work, which we shall try to address elsewhere.

other (*autre*) is the object of his desire, without realizing that the other occupies only imaginarily the place of object *a*. Nobody can be object *a*, except in appearance, in a metaphorical/metonymical sense and for a limited time. Only illusorily can the other satisfy the subject's desire, for he is always inadequate to do so, as is the subject too. This is why Lacan maintains that there is no sexual relationship, that none of the *partenaires* can 'complete' the other, and that "the other half" is no more than an illusion, for none of them has what the other desires and thus has to constantly invent something for the other in love, as well as in art. Lacan goes on to say that there is no harmony between the subject and the object of desire (be it cause or goal), that is, between what the subject believes is the object of his desire and his desire, which accentuates the disharmony or impossibility of the 'sexual relationship'.

Let's now turn to the question of places. Though the Agent is the one who elaborates the discourse, he does so responding to the demands of the other/Other. As we have already said, that Other is not the subject but the network from which he has detached himself in order to emerge. The discourse of the Agent responds then to a demand coming from the Other. The other/Other, insofar as a signifying system, is who interrogates the Agent and the real origin of his discourse. We then have Truth, the foundation of discourse, which the Agent, ignoring or failing to reach it, has to elude as something that escapes his consciousness. As does object *a* (the cause and goal of desire) truth too works as an engine for the signifying change, propelling the search for the impossible *jouissance*. The discourse never states the whole truth; it says less or more, it sometimes says something else, in an endless disparity with what it is meant to say. The fourth place is that of Production, that which is produced by discourse, which has an effect on the other. We shall see how each of the four discourses produces always in disparity with Truth.

The four discourses are arranged in the following algebraic formula[23]:

[23] Lacan rotates the elements in a counterclockwise movement. If we follow that order, the discourse of the Analyst should be placed before the discourse of the Hysteric. However, we have decided to change that order to better appreciate how the discourse

Discourse of the Master

$$\frac{S_1 \rightarrow S_2}{\$ \;//\; a}$$

Discourse of the University

$$\frac{S_2 \rightarrow a}{S_1 \;//\; \$}$$

Discourse of the Hysteric

$$\frac{\$ \rightarrow S_1}{a \;//\; S_2}$$

Discourse of the Analyst

$$\frac{a \rightarrow \$}{S_2 \;//\; S_1}$$

Our task here is to see to what extent these discourses allow us to theoretically think our four dramaturgies. There are several possibilities:

a) That no relationship exists between the four Lacanian discourses and the four dramaturgies. Absurd as though it may seem, the possibility of a non-conceptual relationship between discourses and dramaturgies is worth considering, so that other theoretical approaches can be attempted.

b) That to each Lacanian discourse corresponds a given dramaturgy.

c) That all dramaturgies can be read from each of the four discourses.

d) That despite the above, each dramaturgy has a predominant discourse.

We can now examine each of the four discourses in order to test their possible contributions to our theatrical work.

The Discourse of the Master

This is the starting point, for it poses the condition of the subject as a speaking subject. It is a fundamental discourse coming from the unconscious, the master of our speech—we are spoken by the Other. The Other, as language and culture, imposes ideals on us, marking us with his

of the Analyst is the reverse of the discourse of the Master, and how the discourse of the Hysteric is the reverse of the discourse of the University.

mandates, monitoring our doing. We are captured by desire and the *jouissance* of the Other, from whom we must alienate ourselves in order to enter the social contract. Beyond the clinic and therapy, psychoanalysis invites us to work this alienation in order to emancipate ourselves from the desire and *jouissance* of the Other and access our own desire and *jouissance*—which is not the same as attaining happiness. Psychoanalysis does not provide happiness; rather, it emancipates our desire and *jouissance* so that we can count on having a *savoir* that makes us responsible for our acts, more human, less automated and less controlled by the panoptic.

The agent of this discourse is S_1, the Master signifier, whose meaning depends on an S_2 that signifies it. The Master ignores his castration, he cannot admit it, and this is why $ (and not Truth) is placed below the algorithm's bar. If S_1 as Teacher or Master admitted to being a divided subject instead of a whole one, he would be unfit to occupy that place of dominion, for what he wants is to rule as the owner of the word, the Master of meaning. Let's not forget that every discourse tries to articulate a certain type of bond and social intercourse. What the Teacher professes—or so he thinks and tries to make the others think—is unquestionably true; his obviously illusory pretense is universal validity. The Master speaks as a wholesome One, totalizing and totalitarian, for he seeks to be obeyed, complied with, imitated—which, as we shall see, is an illusion. The purpose of the Teacher as Master or the Master as Teacher as the ruler of meaning is to build a whole, flawless *savoir*, which is why we have S_2 in the place of the other. The other is the Slave, the one who works for the Master's *jouissance* and who must not only comply with the Master but knows how to do it obsequiously:[24] "what is needed is a consent" (*Seminar 17* 29). A pact (not necessarily conscious) exists between Slave and Master. In 1548, when he was only 16 or 18 years old, Étienne de la Boétie wrote an impressive text on voluntary servitude, the echoes of which are

[24] A literal translation of this clause in the original version in Spanish would read: "[the Slave] pampers him—if I am allowed to play with the Lacanian text—when he affirms that in this Master-Slave relationship..." The play of words here is with *consentir*, to consent to, but also to spoil or pamper [Translator's note].

present throughout history and until perhaps Boal's Theater of the Oppressed.[25] Lacan, in a way, warns us that the Master wants everything to work, obviously on his favor, and to attain what he needs to get involved, that is, to consent on losing something: "in exchange for what he loses, he must get back some of the *jouissance*—precisely, the surplus *jouissance*" (*Seminar 17* 113). The discourse of the Master is so successful that it has kept its dominance through the ages, as proved by the fact that "exploited or not, workers work" (*Seminar 17* 181). The way in which humanity has honored work is so great, says Lacan not without irony, that the discourse of the Master has even cancelled (us) "the possibility of not working" (*Seminar 17* 181).

Drawing from Hegel's dialectic of the Master and Slave, with the intermediation of Alexandre Kojève, Lacan positions the Slave as S_2, that is, the other that works and, in so doing, knows Nature. The relationship between power and savoir that these discourses begin to prefigure is obvious. The Master tries to annul the Slave's desire (for freedom), suffocate him under a supposedly total, harmonious *savoir* without contradiction, so as to avoid being questioned by the Slave and, consequently, obtain his obedience. At the place of Production we have *a* since, on working for the Master, the Slave produces objects of *jouissance* (not all of them to satisfy needs). Jouissance, as Lacan would later declare, is useless, good for nothing (*Seminar 20* 11). The surplus *jouissance* (*plus-de-jouir*) appears then as a product of the Slave and as something beyond the law of the Master; it is a complete *jouissance* that neither the Master nor the Slave can ever reach and which is in total disjunction with $\$$.

---

[25] See my essay "Aproximación al Teatro del Oprimido de Augusto Boal. Primera Parte: Resonancias de la servidumbre voluntaria de Étienne de la Boétie" (An Introduction to Augusto Boal's Theater of the Oppressed. Part One: Resonances of Étienne de la Boétie's voluntary servitude), in *Revista Telondefondo*. 35 (January-June 2022).

The discourse of the Master and the dramaturgy of the author

Author → Director
Au/thor* // *Mise-en-scène*

Let us now approach our four dramaturgies from the point of view of the discourse of the Master. Many praxitioners, especially directors, say they comply with the Author's intention and respect the dramatic text. They disapprove of other praxitioners who take liberties in their interpretation and stage the text according to their interests, with no regard for the Author's meaning. Claiming to be "respectful of the dramatic text", faithful to the author dramaturgy, they assume the place of the Master. The Author is thus moved to the place of the Agent, whose word must be heeded. The author's word takes on almost theological qualities: he is the author, the owner of meaning, and treated as though he were a god. There is a religious dimension to the dramaturgy of the author—which will also appear in the dramaturgy of the director—insofar as it maintains a purist relationship to the original text and sees anything diverting from it as heresy.

This is an untenable position, and it would suffice to read Stanislavski, for example, or the testimonies of other directors, to realize that, despite their efforts, there is insecurity at *work* during the staging process over what the "meaning" of the play is; a meaning of which the author is supposedly conscious—something we know is impossible to verify, even if he is alive. There is also a certain degree of infidelity, which grows as time goes by and which manifests itself in various ways. How can we be sure of honoring and reproducing the author's intention? How can we imagine an author as a master who owns the meaning of his own play when he is a divided subject? If we consulted Cervantes, he would tell us that his conscious intention was to parody the romances of chivalry. Were we to be satisfied with such answer, *Don Quixote* would appear to us as an undertaking that has well exceeded its own limits, on account of the enormous critical bibliography it has elicited and continues to elicit, as works of art do, constantly finding new meanings and being the object of ever more writing. But, in reading *Don Quixote*, can we really content ourselves with Cervantes' intention?

As we can see now from the perspective of the discourse of the Master, what the author dramaturgy hides is $\$$, the divided subject: the Author as a divided (castrated) subject with a desire he ignores, a *savoir* that surpasses him. Listening to the anecdotes of many directors as they work on a play of a live author who is present in the rehearsals, a spectrum of reactions from the part of both (but more precisely the author) become evident as they face $\$$ (that is, castration, the existence of a meaning over which they cannot rule and dictate). Under the pressure of the producer, of the author, or of his own conviction as S_2 in the place of the other, the work of the director unfolds amidst the discomfort caused by the unfaithfulness to the word of the Author, the guilt of defiling the dramatic text, and the impossibility of bringing it to the stage in a precise manner. It is interesting to note the frequent paradox of the author being totalitarian towards the director when the former is present, even if his play exposes, for example, the worst horrors of dictatorships and repressive regimes, or works with very controversial issues of feminist discourse.

In such cases, the Author requests that the meaning of the play be blocked and stopped. Some authors excuse themselves and expect this to be done at least for the world premiere. Hidden under the premise of the Author dramaturgy is the assumption of a single reading, the impossibility of which has been proved by many critical studies, psychoanalytic or otherwise. Between the text and its reading there are mediations of all kinds, beginning with the subject and his desire. To postulate a pure, single reading tied to the meaning of the text would be tantamount to claiming that a universal reading is possible, as though the signifier were to rule over the meaning and assume that all readers read through the same lens, the same *fantasme*,[26] ahistorically. In fact, a director or collective who tries to

[26] Though in his *An Introductory Dictionary of Lacanian Psychoanalysis* Dylan Evans translates *fantasme* as 'fantasy', we prefer to keep the original term in French here in order to differentiate it from 'fantasy/phantasy', as used by Freud. The Lacanian term bears subtle but important conceptual differences.

comply with the author's law and illusorily reproduces his discourse progressively and inevitably produces a surplus meaning as the text is being read, worked upon, staged. All kinds of circumstances intervene for this surplus meaning to emerge, and this reveals the untenability of the position of author as owner of meaning of his work. This surplus meaning is a lack of *jouissance* for the Author, as it does not fit into what he claims and dictates. Moreover, this position is at odds with $, for insofar as something emerges beyond what author and praxitioners have said—or believe to have said—there are surprises when the critic comes and says something not recognized by $ and always beyond his conscious discourse.

The Discourse of the University

In this discourse, the position of Agent is occupied by S_2, *savoir*, which the algorithm places over S_1. The Master is absent, though really he is hidden behind Truth. Evidently, Lacan conceives of the discourse of the University as an extension of the discourse of the Master, insofar as it tries to validate S_1, a signifier devoid of meaning, by way of seamless, totalizing philosophical systems, sometimes totalitarian. The role of S_2 is therefore to transmit and propagate truth, the foundation of which lies in the word of an absent Master. As in the previous discourse, here too it is all about an illusory whole *savoir*. According to Lacan, the discourse of the University is that of any church and any bureaucracy. Since *a* occupies the place of the other, what we have is what in Latin America is known after Paulo Freire as "a bank conception of education". This *a* is conceived of as the place of ignorance, a void to be filled with the *savoir* provided by S_2 insofar as transmitter and propagator of the "true" word of the Master. If in the discourse of the Master a *savoir* of the Slave was possible, in the discourse of the University the other is supposed to know nothing. This framework has many pedagogical variants and is a very limited conception of the transmission of *knowledge*, which leaves behind the *savoirs* that, as we have seen, belong in the unconscious, in desire, and in the *jouissance*, pleasure, and pain experienced in the body. This S_2 believes to have a glorious function insofar as it responds to the demand of the other and tries to fill that lack in him with a seamless, universal *savoir*. It tries, as formerly did the Master, to dominate the other's desire, but fails because such desire is impossible to fulfill, its object *a* being unreachable. What it produces instead is just an $\$$, a divided subject captivated by suspicion, in the form of a symptom in which something is manifested, but whose meaning is unknown. S_2 fails in his attempt to seduce, fascinate the other, fill it with his universalizing *savoir*, and because of it $\$$ can no longer identify with S_1. There is, as a result, a sort of disconnection between *savoir* and power in the discourse of the University, as the other realizes that it is not S_2 who speaks but that he is spoken by S_1, the Master. Once again, the produced divided subject, S_2, is perceived as incomplete and therefore as $\$$.

The discourse of the University and the dramaturgy of the director

<u>Direct/tor</u> → <u>Actors/spectator</u>
Author // Mise-e/n-scène

We can now experiment placing the director in the position of the Agent, as representative of the Master and the Teacher. In Latin America, we have very conclusive examples of director-dramaturgy, often superimposed on that of the author, as happens with the discourse of the University, an extension of the discourse of the Master. The director, who in some cases also fulfills pedagogical functions, often tries to sustain the word of the author, presenting himself as the guardian of his word or as the author's representative. He claims, for example, to have studied the author so thoroughly as to being able to consubstantiate with him and therefore he "knows" what the author wanted to say. The often-repeated phrase "Stanislavski is the foundation of every good acting formation" is well known. At the rehearsals, under this illusion of *savoir*, the director/teacher establishes his power as a disciplinary and interpretive protocol that leaves no space to questions about the meaning of a text (dramatic, propaedeutic) he claims to know and respect as nobody else does. In some way, this director continues to be the author's slave, even if he flaunts the pretense of speaking for himself.

But, from another perspective, we can also experiment by placing the director in the position of Agent, as S_2. We would be before a typical director of an author-dramaturgy who addresses actors and technical staff to assert his vision of the play, no matter how far it may be from the author's purpose as S_1. The others, as *a*, have to execute his project as he envisions it, regardless of their opinion. Usually, this is a very experienced director, with a long trajectory and academic studies or practice, who comes to the rehearsal having digested the project and annotated all actors' movements, discussed the project with the stage designer and artists, the music with the music designer, etc. His figure, regardless of his demeanor, is authoritative and unquestionable. The actor, especially if he has come out of a casting by the director, responds to the figure of the character imagined by him long before incarnating a concrete person. The actor is chosen to fit the ideal image of the character formed by the author. The dramatic text or the author as such is under the bar of the algorithm, hidden or silenced. What matters here is the director's staging project, his vision of the play and his *savoir*, which authorize him to justify any kind of departure from or transgression of the original text. He acts as master, but undoubtedly in the name of S_1, who inevitably is there, sometimes even to measure his degree of geniality: if the play is a Shakespeare and the director proposes severe modifications to the original, such transgressions are taken as a mere occurrence, given the fact that the text is known by the community. The novelty of this "latest" Shakespeare requires a traditional Shakespeare, a socially accepted text staged many times—and often classically—according to the discourse of the Master. The spectacle that results from this kind of director who knows everything, who has a command over all the aspects of the staging and for whom his vision of the play is all that matters, is nonetheless an $\$$ that speaks of the unknown *savoir* of the director himself and disjointed from S_1, that is, the original dramatic text or the author. Though certain aspects of Shakespeare are recognizable in the proposal, the critic and/or spectator may find other things linked to the director's *savoir* or appealing to the socio-cultural context in which the spectacle is staged. Be that as it may, in the discourse of the University with the director as Agent there is nothing but an exaggerated whim of the discourse of the Master, for no matter how recognizable Shakespeare might be in the new proposal the truth is that, as we have seen in the discourse of the Master, there is no way to stage an original, single, authentic Shakespeare. Thus both directors, the one who wants to be loyal to Shakespeare's text and the one who rebelliously wants to twist it, transgress it or negate it, are a product of a certain conception of the reading as mediated by multiple historical and cultural factors, of which translation is no less important.

However, we must keep in mind that one thing is to place oneself as director from the discourse of the Master or the University, and another thing is to intend to stage Shakespeare from the discourse of the Hysteric or the Analyst. The power relations involved (between the director and the cast, the audience, and the author) vary greatly. A director positioned in the first option will think of a reading (be it close to the text or transgressive) as "one" truth that belongs to him, which cannot be otherwise and which he wishes to impose on the 'other' (actors, staff, audience). Another thing would be to approach the Shakespearean text as *$* or *a* from the position of Agent, assuming the oracular character of such truth and responding with a conjectural interpretation kind of staging, the truth of which would lie only on its effects. We shall come back to this.

The reproduction of spectacles may be the most evident undertaking of the discourse of the University and its most crass dimension, especially in the case of Broadway musicals. The bureaucratic director adopts here his most evident face. The format is given by an S_1, to whom he responds with obeisance. Undoubtedly, the director is someone chosen by the inter/multinationals for his capacity to command in the name of a project assembled in a foreign metropolitan center. The result is always a product divided between originality and the copy, the foreign and the national. The other, be it the actor or the spectator, must respond to the director's indications, not without suspecting that they respond to an S_1 from another place. The *savoir* at play here seems to be directed to an 'other' who remains unsatisfied, for the original project emerged from a different cultural and socio-political context, leading to the inevitable disjunction, regardless of any provisions, between S_1 and the final $\$$ as result. The production of a London musical in a theater of any Latin American city may be better or worse than the English one, but it will always be an echo, a reproduction, a copy inserted in a differentiated theatrical system and cultural context and, consequently, with a particular reception and a meaning that differs from that in the metropolis.

The discourse of the University and actor training

$$\frac{\text{Instructor}}{\text{Teacher}} \rightarrow \frac{\text{Workshop facilitator}}{\text{Versions}} \qquad // $$

Let us now turn to the discourse of the University from the perspective of actor training. In many universities across the world, actor training is based on the dissemination of a supposedly self-sufficient and complete knowledge. In general terms, we can say that it is based on Stanislavsky's system, regardless of the stage or moment of the Russian master's teachings being adopted: affective memory, physical actions or active analysis (the least known of techniques from the last stages of his career). This corpus of techniques and exercises, of scattered and sometimes contradictory opinions that form the Stanislavsky system in any of its versions, is taken as law in actor practice. A similar situation is found in other instances of training outside the university, where the instructor or director poses himself as the disseminator of the method of another master or teacher, like Grotowski, Strasberg, Barba or Lecoq. In none of these cases is the S_1 in turn presented as an $\$$. The instructor in charge of the discourse of the University (be it in an institution of his own, or in private classes in an actor training workshop) does not look for "hysteric" actors who question *savoir*, but for disciples, repetition devices of a technique or methodology with pretensions of universality and full artistic efficiency. He expects from the disciple's repetition at least a surplus *jouissance* that brings prestige to his teaching. Let's not forget that the teacher here is an Agent of a discourse of which he is not the Master. The debates over who is the most loyal teacher of Stanislavski's methods are well known. Indirectly, the lack of *jouissance* in which he enters is ceded or shared with the Master. In both academia and private workshops, we see that the S_2 in position of Agent presupposes always a Master and hides always that he is really an *\$*, he hides the fact that the Author is not the owner of meaning and therefore he shouldn't rule absolute in matters of art. Or are we to believe that somebody who presents himself as transmitter of the Stanislavsky system cares to think of its faults or its complicity with Capitalism? We mustn't forget that the System is both a scion and an accomplice of Fordism-Taylorism and of Pavlov's experiments with dogs.[27] In a position of ignorance, the disciple receives the recipe of the teacher as gospel, and soon begins to suspect that there is disagreement between the *savoir* of the teacher and that of the Master or author. Thus, the actors' quarrels over the word of the teacher—be it over emotional memory or physical actions—gradually reveal a *\$* that questions the word of S_1.

The discourse of the University and collective creation

Collective	→	Actors/audience
Marx-Brecht-Audience		Dissidence

Contradictory as though it may seem, I risk to position collective creation—at least in its most superficial presentation—within the discourse of the University. The collective degree here depends on the Agent, the one who knows and therefore transmits that knowledge to an 'other' who lacks it. That 'other' may be the newly incorporated members of the collective or the audience, imagined as the people or the masses, to use the

[27] See my essay "Los cuerpos del actor" (The Actor's Bodies).

Foucauldian terms. The members of the collective go on to create research of all kinds or invite specialists on the subject they want to stage. For this reason, they authorize themselves as an S_1 who, at certain moments of revolutionary splendor in Latin America, during the Cuban Revolution and subsequent years, was constituted by Marxist theory, sometimes filtered by Brecht's proposal, or vice-versa. This S_1 could also be the experts who undoubtedly were part of what in general terms we could call here leftist thought with different degrees of revolutionary euphoria of various origins (Stalinist, Maoism, Trotskyism, Guevarism, etc.). However, today we know that few of the groups who made history in the region actually read Marx or Brecht. There was in the air a diluted Marxism and often a second-hand Brechtianism, the variations of which depended on the opinions held by the local Communist Party (based on the S_1 of the Soviet quarters), the Trotskyist dissidence, or those who followed the Leninist, Guevarist or Maoist mandates. Positioned on the place of Truth and supported by the knowledge produced by science, this S_1 (Marxism, Brechtianism, the Party) imagined the production of a spectacle that could scientifically transcend the veil of ideology and expose by way of an eloquent narrative the hidden laws of Capitalist economic and socio-political dominance. They methodically collected evidence, interviewed any person related to the subject, resorted to whatever discipline or expert they could find and, by way of improvisation, went on adjusting the narrative sequences of the spectacle to this accumulated knowledge for the benefit of a supposedly ignorant audience. However, the conjectural, based on another kind of truth, another kind of *savoir* of a more oracular kind, either escaped them or were consciously rejected for its counter-revolutionary nature,[28] and this is why today the majority of those plays look completely insipid and unfortunately limited to an already surpassed juncture in history. Such texts remain in the annals of theater just as a symptom of an historical era. In lacking that 'other' truth of an oracular nature (that un-

[28] A long account of the conflictive relations between Marxism and psychoanalysis in Latin America, with a voluminous bibliography, could be inserted here. Suffice it to say that Freudian thought had already been stigmatized since before the Russian Revolution.

known *savoir*) such plays fail to interrogate us today, for they lack the artistic potential to travel through history. They remain as testimony of a shining era of Latin American theater, conceived as they were by instruments or tools to an end that was political, not artistic. Such is the destiny of all *agit-prop* art. However, in some of them—those that happened to produce an interesting $\$$—some dimension of the repressed can still be detected, which continues to foster meaning and to insist in our historical-social experience. I invite the reader to read, for example, the three versions of *El Paraíso recobrao* (Recovered Paradise) by the Cuban theater group Escambray. Every review of a new version was subjected to an increased censorship (including self-censorship), to the point that the last two versions--which today have no other value than as documents for historical debate—ended up eliminating the fascinating and controversial allegory of the leaders of the Cuban Revolution and their ways of imagining the exercise of power—an unintended effect, it seems, though probably very attractive to the audience in its first version.[29]

It may well be that the constant dissidences that gradually fragmented the collective creation groups stemmed from the production of $\$$. More than a question of the exercise of power, the discourse of the University that inspired these experiences—paradoxically, except for the Cuban case, all of them emerging at the margins of State bureaucracy—reproduced the bureaucratic character so typical of the lucid lefts, for which there is always an S_1 in disjunction with an $\$$ difficult to approach and control. Many of the artists that participated of these experiences, as well as the audience to which they were addressed, were neither in the place of eminent ignorance assigned to them by the groups, nor in a situation to accept the indoctrination through theater, so that they ended up dissenting from the proposal by creating their own groups or forgetting the spectacle altogether. As far as I know, with the exception of the interesting *Guadalupe años cincuenta* (Guadalupe in the Fifties) of the Colombian Candelaria

[29] See my reading of *El Paraíso recobrao* in chapter V of my *Theatricality and Political Experience in Latin America*, the first version of which appeared in the *Latin American Theater Anthology* (1950-2007) compiled by Lola Proaño and Gustavo Geirola.

group, none of the texts published or produced by collective creation groups was restaged. In the case of *Guadalupe*, the restaging was by the same group, and not without certain conviction that it was a memory (almost museographical) exercise.

The Discourse of the Hysteric

Lacan names this discourse after the hysteric women on whom Freud founded psychoanalysis—which does not mean that there are no hysteric males or, as many have said, that the feminine noun is used by Lacan in a pejorative, male-supremacist sense. In this discourse, we have $\$$ in the position of Agent. We have already said that this is a divided subject, unaware of his desire and aspiring to a *savoir* that must come from the Master (whoever assumes that place, a dangerous one for the analyst and, to a certain extent, for the theater director too). Though the hysteric demands this *savoir* and assumes that the analyst occupies the place of S_1 (a subject supposed to know), she does not cease to invalidate his interventions, especially when these are presented as S_2 (that is, in the form of totalizing explanations). As we shall later see, the analyst must half-tell the truth, present it as an enigma, so that the hysteric can go on with her discourse. As a subject of the unconscious,[30] the hysteric ignores the foundation of her desire, does not know what her symptoms say nor does she understand what her dreams, lapses, jokes and other equivocations reveal, and thus demands this *savoir* (S_2) over her destiny to a supposedly knowing subject (S_1) whom she imagines as whole, *authorized*. Lacan reminds us that what the hysteric wants is a master and risks the hypothesis that maybe this is where "the invention of the master began" (*Seminar 17* 137). Be that as it may, the hysteric wants a master, but one "over whom she

[30] Obviously, men are not excluded, especially if they are mystics, capable of placing themselves, like women, on the side of the not-all (*Seminar 20* 92) in the formulae of sexuation. Lacan did not intend to leave out men by using the feminine to name this discourse. Beyond paying homage to Freud's patients, without whom psychoanalysis would not have been founded, the relationship between women and *jouissance* is a very complex one, into which we cannot delve here.

can reign. She reigns and he doesn't govern" (*Seminar 17* 137). The formula of this discourse shows us an important disjunction between the *savoir* produced by S_1 as an answer (that is, S_2) and object *a*, the cause of the hysteric's desire. This S_2 fails to satisfy her, make her whole, and thus she continues demanding. The discourse of the Hysteric dramatizes desire; the primeval dissatisfaction whose main task it is "the promotion of dissatisfied desire" (*Seminar 17* 78). The hysteric, in a way, mistakes S_1 for the signifier of her destiny and her dissatisfaction with a reply that contains S_2 but fails to comprehend *a* makes her see the Master (the S_1) as impotent. This *a* in the place of Truth cannot be included *into* or captured *by* the Master's *savoir*. Thus, the hysteric—in her industriousness, as Lacan defines her—models a nonconformist subject that signals the impotence of the Master and the impotence of the *savoir* of both S_1 and S_2. She, who seeks a Master, wants to make known that language "falls short of comprehending the vastness of what she, as woman, can display in respect of *jouissance*" (*Seminar 17* 35). The hysteric, moreover, wants that the other, whom she calls man, "knows how precious she is as an object in the context of this discourse" (*Seminar 17* 35). This is about a *savoir* that proves impotent in dealing with desire, and thus we can say that desire is uneducable.[31] For us *praxitioners*, it is interesting to cite Lacan when he says that the discourse of the Hysteric "exists and would exist in any case, with or without psychoanalysis" (*Seminar 17* 33) for, in a way, just as the psychoanalyst is the "hysterization of discourse…in artificial conditions" (*Seminar 17* 33), the task of the *praxitioner*, as artist—and not necessarily that of theater-making—can be conceived in the same terms.

The discourse of the Hysteric and collective creation

$$\frac{\text{Collec/tive}}{\text{People-Audience}} \quad \rightarrow \quad \frac{\text{Marx-Brecht-Party-People-Audience}}{\textit{Mise-en-scène}}$$

[31] Following Freud's line, for Lacan to govern, educate, analyze, and cause to desire are real (and therefore impossible) operations or professions (*Seminar 17* 179, 186-7).

In the framework of this discourse in particular, we could place the actor and another kind of director in the place of the Agent. However, before doing so, let us go back to the question of the dramaturgy of collective creation, which we had already explored in the discourse of the University section. To approach collective creation from the discourse of the Hysteric offers a different perspective, more tragic, in a way, than it is from the discourse of the University. Let's position the collective in the place of the Agent, which in the discourse of the Hysteric is $, the divided subject that knows nothing about her desire and demands this *savoir* from the other, who in this discourse happens to be S_1, the Master signifier. Which Master is the collective addressing? As we have seen in the previous discourse, the two great Masters to whom people appealed in the 1960s were, thinking from authorship, Marx and Brecht, in any of their variants. They do not work here as guarantors of *savoir*, as we saw in the discourse of the University, but as 'other' on whom the demand for (political) savoir is placed. We also said that the members of the collective who had read and studied these German authors were few and, therefore, the collective incited its members to conduct the readings and discuss them in various formats. Obviously, the demand to Marx was not about a desire for theatrical knowledge, for which Brecht was there. Both authors, however, could not respond for collective desire, not because they were not alive—as in the case of the Analyst in their place—but because access to them was already stigmatized by several interpretations and censorship coming from the very center of the political left. Marx and Brecht always responded from their writings and, as we have seen to happen always in the discourse of the Master, if they *appeared* to do it, it was under the figure of a guide, a manual or a confirmation of what supposedly the collective believed to know about them—that is, the Masters responded in the worst possible way as the worst of analysts, presenting themselves as models or ideals to obey, not to question.

It is possible to imagine another Master for the collective, another living S_1 regarded as the knower of everything and related to the desire of *praxitioners*: the audience, the people (the ultimate sovereign). As we all know, the audience was probed and debates were opened at the end of the show, which lead to exhaustive reviews of the spectacles. Having demanded the group's theatrical response, the audience as S_1 in the place of the other had the last word. It was placed as a S_2, a subject of supposed *savoir* from whom a total response was expected over the group's destiny, the object *a*, the cause of collective desire who, as the disjunction in the algorithm shows, was condemned to not know. Augusto Boal's Theater of the Oppressed, especially in its first stage before exile in Europe, is an eloquent example of this discourse. As the audience in the place of the other as S_1 shows, it was not about (as in the previous discourse) transmitting a *savoir* founded on leftist thought, or about knowing the members of the audience or the people, but demanding from the audience a *savoir* on collective desire. The question of power underlying all these discourses cannot be ignored. Viewed from the perspective of the discourse of the Hysteric, collective creation appears in the place of the Agent as getting authorization from the audience, but at the same time wanting to dominate it, as though they needed to have a Master not to obey him, but to reign over him.

But what audience-people had collective members in their minds? Just as the hysteric mistakes S_1 for her destiny, the collective believes that the people are their destiny. Playing with the Lacanian irony on the invention of the Master in the discourse of the Hysteric, it is possible to presume that "the people", as part of a faceless mass, totally homogeneous and oppressed as the collective imagined them, did not exist and has even been an imaginary construction, an invention of the collective itself. It is not by chance that more recently subaltern studies, feminism, cultural studies, queer theory, and minority studies have brought a less homogeneous idea of the audience-people. The savoir that S_1 produces in response to S_2 is not enough for the audience, does not make it whole or satisfy its demand for *savoir* about its desire, and so the collective resumes its task with a new demand to S_1, of which surely another S_2 will emerge in the form of a new spectacle. The paradox here is the fact that, being in the place of the Agent, the collective wants to dominate the other, the audience, proposing a spectacle that shows the real face of the economic structure and Capitalist domination hidden by ideology (which supposedly the people ignore) but at the same time supports the people as S_1, as Master of a whole *savoir*. As we have seen, the *savoir* thus produced does not satisfy the collective's desire, namely (as expressed in the words used at the time) liberation from capitalist oppression, the foundation of a new man, and socialism. The people do not respond with the *savoir* about *a* (which is located in the place of truth) and so the collective, in its industriousness, suspects that the people must be impotent, that is, too alienated to say anything about that *a*, which, as we know, cannot be captured by any *savoir*. Thus, the collective, in the discourse of the Hysteric, ends up permanently discontented, dissatisfied with total *savoir* as well as with the Master, and abandons its initial pedagogical impulse as soon as its members realize that desire (one's own, anybody's, even that of the audience-people) is uneducable. And this is going to produce a new *savoir*, a new S_1, which, in the case of our dramaturgies, could be thought of as the current actor-dramaturgy.

The discourse of the Hysteric and the dramaturgy of the director

<u>Director</u>	→	<u>Actors-Audience</u>
Mise-en-scène		Improvisation

There is another modality of director-dramaturgy that could also be thought of from the discourse of the Hysteric. It is the director who, in the position of Agent as $\$$, arrives to the rehearsal with more doubts than certainties. In the place of the other we see S_1 incarnated in the actors and the team, whom the director venerates and from whom he expects to get back a *savoir* over his desire. It is difficult to find this modality in commercial theater; the directors that put themselves in this position (though not in the pure form we present here) often work with independent theater. Often being actors themselves, the directors of this kind go to the rehearsal having just read the text and with no idea as to how the staging will be conducted. They prefer to build it step by step drawing from the improvisation work with actors, from whom they expect a lot. This director believes that the actors are the ones who really know what he wants to do; it is in the improvisation work where the actors give him back—or so he expects—the *savoir* about his object *a*. He runs the risk, obviously, of staging what his actors suggest him by way of improvisations, as though it were a gospel. Usually this doesn't happen, precisely because, being a *$*, his strategy is, as we have seen, to find a master that does not govern, and over whom he can rule. In a way, he seeks in his actors the authorization and authority he needs for that, and consequently he somehow invents them as master. The S_2 he proposes by his actors is not completely satisfactory and thus he keeps his position as *$* for as long as there is a disjunction between what the actors provide and the cause of his desire. This forces him to return to the demand once and again, and this is why in this type of framework theatrical work can last very long. The director always feels that there is something the discourse and the *savoir* of his actors fail to capture, and hence his constant dissatisfaction. Even after the premiere, he feels that work must continue—industriousness being part of the character of the hysteric—and therefore he never ceases to program more adjustment rehearsals. Since his actors never really satisfy him, the director may resort to the audience as S_1, organizing previews or question-answer sessions after each show, which do nothing but turn him back to the demand again. However, in acting this way, the director has the possibility of letting out a new S_2 who opens up a new period of his trajectory or that of the theater paradigm. This type of director, who usually turns into a master or an eccentric and admired figure, manages to make actors, critics, and audience members in his theatrical environment aware of what he means for the theater culture of his city or country, as though he were that "precious object" of which Lacan talked referring to the hysteric.

A brief excurse on savoir

It is now time to approach, albeit very briefly, the question of *savoir* before entering the discourse of the Analyst. There is "a *savoir not known*"

(*Seminar 17* 33), says Lacan. He also declares that psychoanalysis is on the side of *savoir* and not of knowledge. We can't delve into it here but suffice it to say that this declaration has definitive consequences in the way psychoanalysis is understood as a discipline. This *savoir* of which Lacan speaks is a network (*Seminar 17* 11) of signifiers. Lacan also talks of the "*savoir* about the *jouissance* of the Other" (*Seminar 17* 12), of "the body of the other, which symbolizes it" (*Seminar 20* 12). He then adds: "*savoir* is what makes life stop at a certain limit before *jouissance*" (*Seminar 17* 17). This is how the role of the *fantasme* must be understood, protecting the subject from *jouissance*, as can be appreciated in the famous *fantasme* formula *$◊a*, where the rhomboid or lozenge operates as a screen before object *a*. This corpus of citations may elicit many questions in the field of theater. Instead of trying to enter into detail here, we shall limit ourselves to tackle one aspect that can help us in our work with the four discourses and the four dramaturgies.

There is, in effect, a conscious *savoir*, but what Freud discovers when he works with hysteric women is the unconscious, which Lacan presents as structured *as* a language (and not *by* it, he makes it clear). The unconscious is structured "as the sets in set theory, as letters" (*Seminar 20* 62). From the Hegelian perspective, the old Slave is characterized as "the support of *savoir*" (*Seminar 17* 17) and the Master only lives off of what his Slave produces for his *jouissance*, with no need for *savoir*. The Slave possesses know-how; however, this is not enough to found a *savoir* that knows itself, that is self-conscious, an *episteme*. When Plato—Lacan reminds us, following Nietzsche—makes the Slave talk guided by the precise questions as formulated by the Master, he dwells on the issue of "the robbery, the kidnapping, the subtraction of savoir to slavery by the Master's operation" (*Seminar 17* 20) and he distinguishes articulated, transmissible *savoir* from know-how, which, although not completely lacking articulation by language, is akin to the animal instinct, inasmuch as instinct is a form of *savoir*, the automatic *savoir* (*savoir-faire*) of life in animals as well as in humans. Let's not forget however that humans are what they are not for their instinct but for the drive and for desire.[32] *Episteme* is then transmissible *savoir*, once it has passed—says Lacan jokingly—from the pocket of the Slave into the pocket of the Master, as though it were "a bank transfer" (*Seminar 17* 22). *Episteme* is the *savoir* of the Master; it is science, "a *savoir* completely autonomous from mythical *savoir*" (*Seminar 17* 94). Science "rejects and excludes the dynamics of truth" (*Seminar 17* 95); it is a *savoir* that suppresses what dwells in mythical *savoir*, a "disjointed *savoir* as we find it in the unconscious" (*Seminar 17* 95), and this is why psychoanalysis interrogates science. From the Master's perspective, the discourse of the unconscious seems to utter nonsense, but it is in this senseless *savoir*,[33] unconscious of itself and which cannot offer its fundamentals, where *jouissance* resides and where Lacan's work is located (*Seminar 17* 86). *Jouissance* is constantly being produced by the discourse of the Master and the pseudo-discourse of Capitalism, and consequently S_1 "not only does not induce but it determines, castration" (*Seminar 17* 93). Lacan will keep this oracular version of the word in analysis, and consequently the Freudian relationship between myth and truth too. In *Seminar 18* he will implicitly refer to Freud's 1937 essay on the constructions in psychoanalysis. As we know, the analysand's acceptance of an interpretation does not confirm its exactitude; it is not a question of true or false as in logic. What the analyst's interpretation confirms are the after-effects it may have on the analysand (new lapses, new dreams, etc.). This is why Lacan defines psychoanalysis as a conjectural science, and tells us:

---

[32] Although Freud supervised to a certain extent the translation into Spanish of his work by López Ballesteros, the translation of *Trieb* (drive) as 'instinct' created tremendous confusion. Therefore, in its later edition, Editorial Amorrortu made sure to differentiate *Trieb* from *Instinkt*.

[33] In *Seminar 20*, Lacan insists on the fact that "the subject is not the one who thinks. The subject is rather the one whom we oblige not to say everything, which is what we say to him to please him—it is impossible to say everything—but to say nonsense [instead, since] with these nonsensical utterances we are going to conduct the analysis, and thus enter into the new subject of the unconscious" (*Seminar 20* 31). This is related to the silly signifier that Lacan mentions in the same Seminar, and constitutes a gateway to the practice of improvisation at the theatrical rehearsal from the discourse of the Hysteric. From director-dramaturgy to collective creation (both based on the discourse of the University), improvisation varies greatly.

> If, having taken its titles of nobility from it the analytic experience, [psychoanalysis] finds itself involved in the Oedipal myth, it is because it preserves the emphatic enunciation of the oracle and, moreover, because the interpretation remains always on the same level. It is only true on account of its consequences, exactly the same as the oracle. The interpretation is not submitted to a truth-test that settles for a yes or a no, rather it triggers the truth as such. It is only true to the extent that it is truly followed. (*Seminar 18* 13)

Though in the Platonic dialogues the questions the Master poses the Slave are derisory—the answers to which are somehow implied in them, as a way to demonstrate that the Slave knows what he doesn't know (*Seminar 17* 159)—they fulfill the objective of snatching *savoir* from the Slave. In some way, the Master is capable of formulating and imposing the rules of this dialogue—as it often happens during a theater rehearsal or can be observed in Strasberg—by transferring them to an epistemic discourse that obviously confirms his initial idea. Lacan shows us to this effect that the Master knows and that *jouissance* is not his privilege, and so it remains to be seen "how the Slave's position in *jouissance* is articulated" (*Seminar 17* 21). The Slave's *savoir* has thus been transformed into that of the Master, an ill-gotten *savoir* that exists more in theory than in practice and which fails to turn itself into an effective dominion over the Slave until it is turned into a science, that is, when "the subject's function in the strict S_1 to S_2 relation" is extracted, an operation conducted by Descartes (*Seminar 17* 21).

The pseudo-capitalist discourse[34]

If philosophy is the old discourse of the Master, science is the discourse of the modern Master, closer to the discourse of the University and, via this, an accomplice of today's neoliberalism, as we can see in the pseudo-capitalist discourse Lacan added to his four discourses. The capitalist discourse is a pseudo-discourse because instead of promoting social bonds it tends to dissolve them, disintegrate them, with precise political and devastating effects for the community. In the discourse of the modern Master, the surplus *jouissance* is acknowledged, counted, calculated, totalized, thus putting in motion "what is called capital accumulation" (*Seminar 17* 192). Lacan would later provide the formula of capitalist discourse, another style of the discourse of the Master (*Seminar 17* 180).

Capitalist discourse

$$\underline{\$} \rightarrow \underline{S_2}$$

$$S_1 \; // \; a$$

Philosophy, which has expropriated *savoir* from the Slave and founded the *savoir* of the Master (*Seminar 17* 159), is a useful weapon because it fascinates the Slave, but it loses its effectiveness before science, the articulated signifier; it loses its fascinating capacity for the benefit of the modern Master. Since *savoir* is understood here as "a means for *jouissance*" (*Seminar 17* 284), and since "the Slave is the sole owner of the means of *jouissance*" (*Seminar 17* 84), it is no longer possible to maintain that work

[34] We shall not dwell on this discourse here. Alternatively, the reader may consult two of my essays: "Justicia, neoliberalismo y extimidad: A propósito de *Hambre*, de Merly Macías" (Justice, neoliberalism and extimacy: About *Hunger*, by Merly Macías) and "Patriarcado, crimen y sociedad postedípica en dos obras de Hugo Salcedo: Hacia un teatro de emancipación" (Patriarchy, crime and post-Oedipal society in two works by Hugo Salcedo: Towards a theater of emancipation).

* *Extimité* is a neologism created by Lacan (see Evans, Dylan. *An Introductory Dictionary of Lacanian Psychoanalysis*, Routledge, London/New York, 2006, p. 59 [Translator's Note].

produces *savoir* ("no work ever engendered *savoir*" [*Seminar 17* 84]),[35] neither is it possible to affirm that either the Master or the Slave have a desire for *savoir* that leads to it—which presents serious consequences for the pedagogic discourse we often assume without questioning. The Master only wants things to work, "that the thing goes" (*Seminar 17* 22); he does not need *savoir*. However, what leads him to *savoir* is the discourse of the Hysteric who shows her fault to the Master, opening the possibility for new questions, new S_1s. Therefore, neither the discourse of the Master, nor the discourse of the University lead to savoir as a means to *jouissance*; they at the most lead to knowledge, the transmission of an *episteme* that is indifferent to truth.

In this very brief and cursory excurse we have attempted to establish a way to think of theatrical praxis as an art that, rather than being indifferent to truth, bases its political position in dealing with *jouissance*, for the truth in the discourse of the Master, rather than hidden, is *compressed*, and therefore "it has to be deployed in order to be legible" (*Seminar 17* 83). We have somehow founded here a dialogue between psychoanalysis and a theatrical praxis capable of proposing spectacles in which truth is deployed by the letter; not to be contemplated or heard, as a dogma, but read and listened to—operations both fundamental to the discourse of the Analyst. The relationship between the *praxitioner* and the audience is akin to that of the analyst and the analysand who deals with an 'other' that has no interest in knowing the truth of his desire (*Seminar 17* 67).[36] As the analyst, the *praxitioner* is expected not to tell the truth—which is impossible—but "to make his *savoir* work as a word of truth. It is precisely because of this that he limits himself to half-saying" (*Seminar 17* 56). In his *Television*, Lacan states that it is "materially impossible" to say the whole truth, for lack of words, and he adds; "It is precisely for this impossibility that

[35] This reference must obviously be debated, for in some way it seems to contradict what Lacan always emphasized in relation to the unconscious as a *savoir* that thinks and even works, and therefore we talk of the "dream-work" (*Television* 97).

[36] Lacan works conceptually on the differences between need, demand, desire and *jouissance*. It is imperative to discuss these questions as they appear in theatrical praxis. I made a first attempt in my essay "La praxis teatral y lo político: la demanda, el teatrista y el público" (Theatrical praxis and the political: demand, the *praxitioner* and the audience).

truth aspires to the real" (83). Semiotics, as a science, cannot help its own determination: in its quest for systematic categorization it can never understand that 'the truth' of a dramatic or spectacular text appears always as transcending its boundaries.

The Discourse of the Analyst

Discourse of the Analyst

$$\frac{a}{S_2} \rightarrow \frac{\$}{S_1}$$

$$S_2 \; // \; S_1$$

As the formula indicates, the discourse of the Analyst is the reverse of the discourse of the Master. The analyst occupies the place of the Agent as the semblance of *a* for the barred subject [*$*], and thus we see S_1 in the place of Production. Having given up any pretense of domination or legislation, S_1 leaves the Master signifier disjointed from S_2. The analyst, says Lacan, tries to occupy the place of the Agent as an *a* that determines its discourse, precisely to indicate that "he is by no means there of his own accord" (*Seminar 17* 56), but rather he is "where the surplus *jouissance* was, the *jouir* of the other, where I, as promoter of the psychoanalytic act, must arrive" (*Seminar 17* 56). However, there is no way to question, evoke, approach or elaborate *a* as *jouissance* except from a semblance, that is, an image that acts as wrapping or cloak of object *a* (*Seminar 20* 112). When *a* is in the place of the semblance and the analyst plays dead, he refrains from legislating and from trying to dominate the desire of *$* but frustrates the demand the latter directs at him as a subject of supposed *savoir*. Moreover, when responding with enigmas, with the half-telling of the truth, the analyst propitiates that the other perceive himself as *$* leaving the possibility open for new dreams, lapses, and stumbles. In this sense, the one who analyzes is the analysand, for the discourse of the Analyst is installed precisely to allow the subject to confront the holes in his own discourse.

Lacan points out that the position of the analyst is a difficult one, but this is where psychoanalysis rests: the discourse of the Analyst "must find itself on the opposed side of any will, at least manifestly, to dominate. I say *at least manifestly* not because he has to conceal it, but because, after all, it is easy to shift back towards the discourse of domination" (*Seminar 17* 73). The analysand, the divided subject, supposes that the analyst has some *savoir* over his desire, a *savoir* that is going to complete or fill up that lack-of-being (his *a*), which the cause of desire. But the analyst does not respond to that demand because, as we see, the bar in the algorithm separates it from S_2; the analyst in position of Agent as *a* cannot place himself as the analysand's ideal (the Ideal ego) neither can he give him the impression of possessing a truth over his desire. Since the analyst refuses to put himself in the position of Master, his function is to respond with enigmas in order to frustrate the analysand's demands for meaning and keep him working on his desire by deposing the masks that trap him and alienate him. "We are—says Lacan, thinking of analysts—there to make him know all he knows he doesn't know" (*Seminar 17* 119). This is why the analyst does not offer the analysand an image of *savoir* and power, lest he once more get trapped and alienate himself or, worse even, try to imitate the analyst. On the contrary, being in the position of *a*, the analyst evokes the unattainable surplus *jouissance* and returns the analysand the basic questions of who he is and who is speaking through him. Therefore, S_2 in the place of Truth operates (also) as the unconscious *savoir* of the analysand.

When confronting him with the half-telling of the enigma —"half telling is the internal law of all types of truth enunciations" (*Seminar 17* 116)— the analyst places the analysand again in the position of facing his own lack-of-being and get rid of the images that have captivated him. Lacan thinks that psychoanalysis proposes this "reckless operation [as it] commits to follow the track of the desire for *savoir*" (*Seminar 17* 112), inviting the analysand to say anything: "Come, say anything that comes to mind, no matter how fragmented it is, how much it shows that you don't think or are nothing at all, the thing may work, and whatever it produces will always be received" (*Seminar 18* 112). Obviously, the truth to which the analysand has access does not have to be always beneficial (*Seminar 17*

112), but Lacan additionally states that S_2 (inasmuch as corpus of savoir of psychoanalysis, as shown by the algorithm) has to stay suspended in a way. It is not about applying universalizing formulae before $\$$, for every analysand is a case and the analyst proceeds case by case. And each case may put parts of the theory in dire straits, as happened to Freud. Neither is it about "applying" psychoanalysis (an impossible task), but rather about confronting each case to rethink theory. This theory is not a *model* that straightjackets the object, nor is it a theory that corroborates the truth of the object, but a theory localized in the epistemic context of discovery, of creativity and invention, and thus we can work with psychoanalysis in theatrical praxis.

The discourse of the Analyst and the dramaturgy of the actor

Which of our four dramaturgies could be adjusted or brought closer to the discourse of the Analyst? This is a difficult question. Considering what we have so far discussed here, if we were to pose the idea of a dramaturgy from an Agent in a position of power, we would conclude that none of the four dramaturgies has the ability to exemplify the discourse of the Analyst. Though uncommon, the inverse proposition is also possible, namely that an author, director or group were to admit putting themselves in the position of *a*, and reject power. As the semblance of *a* in the discourse of the Analyst, the position of the Agent is difficult to maintain, though not impossible. However, this doesn't seem to be common in theatrical praxis. As Freud declares in his technical essays: "I don't mean to claim that it is always easy for the physician to keep within the confines of ethics and technique" (*O. C.* 12: 172).

Should we now intend to do justice to the dramaturgy of the actor, we would have to begin by defining it and asking whether it is the closest one to the discourse of the Analyst. The word 'justice' here takes meaning from a historical perspective: ever since the beginning of the seventeenth century, at the dawn of Western modernity, the actor has been kept outside the *creative* theatrical process. He had, for very long, to submit to the word of the author and the text, later to the projects and mandates of the *régisseur* or director and, finally, in a more democratic context, to the difficult dynamics of the group or collective. Within variable margins of action, his function has been limited to that of *interpreter*. A good part of acting training is directed to model this professional capable of attaining, in the minimum time and with the maximum efficacy, the results expected by a production, the parameters of which and its economic, aesthetic, and political benefits being, in general, alien to him.

When talking of collective creation, we have seen how the figure of the actor takes on certain preponderance from the perspective of the discourse of the University and the discourse of the Hysteric. However, we are now confronted—as we were at the beginning of this essay—with the need to discuss some questions linked to the actor-dramaturgy, which, at least historically, are connected to collective creation. Leaving aside the temptation to dwell on the extensive bibliography available on this topic—not always bent on defining its own terms—we shall try to specify some necessary questions in order to imagine the possibility of a dramaturgy conceived within the dimension of the discourse of the Analyst. The distinction Patrice Pavis makes between collective creation and creative collective may be of use here. Pavis defines creative collective as "a collectivity of meaning and a collective subject of theatrical enunciation" (63). In a way, this creative collective may include every performative community expression. The question had already been approached by Platon Michailovich Keržencev (1881-1940) in his book *Il Teatro Creativo. Teatro proletario negli anni '20 in Rusia*, where he poses the need to open a space for collective creativity during the Russian Revolution; a way to give theater a use value making expressive activity accessible to all. This tendency would later develop into what we know as community theater.[37] Collective creativity would then be a generalized form of the actor-dramaturgy, though its results cannot be obtained without an organization—in general, a pyramidal one—of the show's production.

---

[37] See "La creación colectiva y el teatro creativo en la perspectiva de Platon Michailovic Keržencev y la Revolución Rusa" (Creative collection and creative theater in the perspective of Platon Michailovic Keržencev and the Russian Revolution) included in the 'Addendum' section of this essay.

As for the dramaturgy of the actor in the more confined field of theatrical praxis, we can turn to the definition offered by Eugenio Barba at the ninth session of the ISTA in May 1995:

> Actor-dramaturgy means, above all, the ability to build the equivalent of the complexity that characterizes actions in life. This construction, perceived as a character, must have a sensorial and mental impact on the spectator. The objective of the actor-dramaturgy is the ability to stimulate affective reactions.[38]

Though it assumes the form of a definition, the meaning of this broad and somehow traditional approach is rather ambiguous and quite imprecise insofar as is based on undefined theoretical terms and depends on a supposed understandability on the part of the reader. However, when posed within the framework of a reflection over acting exercises and physical actions, the Barbian definition is oriented to the work of the actor in order to obtain a psychological effect on the spectator. As we shall later see, while for Barba the spectator "reacts", for Buenaventura the spectator "modifies" the spectacle. For Boal, however, in assuming the functions of the *spect-actor*, the audience turns into the doer/maker, not without consequences. We are here confronted by two conflicting conceptions of the subject. If Barba's technical approach to the actor and his body is valid in its almost Pavlovian context of instrumentation, it can bring little light onto our psychoanalysis work field, despite its use of the term "construction"—which also appears in the Freudian vocabulary.

The dramaturgy of the actor, historically invisible under those of author and director, began to emerge again in the twentieth century. When contrasted to the latter two, this dramaturgy is often related to collective creation, which in turn brings the ideas of improvisation and writing to the fore. Evidently, in his own way, the actor produces dramaturgy—even

[38] See Eugenio Barba's essay "Un amuleto hecho de memoria. El significado de los ejercicios en la dramaturgia del actor" (An amulet made of memory. The meaning of exercises in the dramaturgy of the actor).

if he is not aware of it. But since it doesn't respond to a single conception, this dramaturgy often lacks clarity and is again threatened by the other two. Improvisation, one of the areas historically more closely linked to the actor's practice, may even be appropriated by the author. According to Mauricio Kartun, the author "effects a sort of imaginary improvisation in which he perceives—simultaneously and paradoxically—through his own eyes and through the senses of the incarnated characters."[39] The idea of writing is also expanded here: it is no longer limited to the writing of a verbal text, and the *staging*, conceived as a score,[40] is thought of in terms of a stage score in which multiple artists would creatively participate, among them the actor. Collective creation, moreover, has been thought of in multiple ways and, as we shall see, it is not a emerging product, as Patrice Pavis posed in his *Dictionary of Theater* back in the 1960s.

---

[39] In Gabriela Borgna, "To write in an excited space and body", cited by María Fernanda Pinta in "Dramaturgia del actor y técnicas de improvisación. Escrituras teatrales contemporáneas" (Actor-dramaturgy and improvisation techniques. Contemporary theatrical writings).

[40] The idea of a stage score, which would define the show, comes fundamentally from Stanislavski and, above all, from Meyerhold. With it, an attempt is made to bring the staging closer to the music. It has also served to try to conceptualize the actor's practice. Thus, the idea of subscore arises from the subtext, as Stanislavski (and Barba) proposed, in an attempt to include the kinesthetic, the gestural, the physical actions, the emotional, etc. Obviously, the actor would be the one who assumes authorship here. The score includes non-verbal languages and this complicates its writing. However, semiotics has achieved little or nothing—especially when limited to its role of sign—in reaching a writing equivalent to a musical writing to account for the multiple codes and languages involved in the staging. Perhaps these issues should be taken up from the signifier. Lacan takes up the idea of score and polyphony from his reading of Levi-Strauss, Søren Kierkegaard and Freud, in relation to repetition; to the voice as object *a*, silence, to the Saussurean anagram, the letter and other concepts of analytical praxis. An investigation into these issues in theatrical praxis remains to be done.

The dramaturgy of the Actor and collective creation

Maybe the most brilliant and illuminating text I have so far read on actor-dramaturgy is "La dramaturgia de actor" (Actor-dramaturgy), by Colombian author Enrique Buenaventura, Cali, 1985.[41] This excellent text is an ideal tool to answer some questions about our endeavor here, namely to discuss the actor-dramaturgy from the discourse of the Analyst. Buenaventura's enthusiasm for theatrical semiotic studies, so much in vogue at the time, lead him to differentiate between dramatic literature and theater, in the understanding that only the former can be thought of as a literary genre. Theater, for its part, is a spectacle, and verbal language is only one among the many languages (visual, sound) that take part in a staging. Theater "is no more and no less than the ephemeral moment in which a relationship between actors and spectators is produced". And though Buenaventura does not hide his enthusiasm for a theatrical semiotics then regarded as promising, he does not fail to recognize the problematic involved: what would be the use of a semiotic analysis of such an ephemeral and unrepeatable entity as the theatrical act? Would it be necessary to carry out a semiotic analysis at every show?

Buenaventura's queries are very close to what psychoanalysis had to face as a discipline: on the one hand, the need to establish a theory and a technique and, on the other, the realization that it is impossible to generalize and universalize, and that the procedure must operate on a case-by-case basis. Each analysand leads the analyst to rethink the theory in its entirety and suspend his knowledge in order to listen. Psychoanalysis cannot be 'applied'—a rather unfortunate term much in use (and abuse) in academia. The same happens with theater: though its basic structure "gives the impression of remaining intact", the spectacle (including the actor) is *modified* each time by the spectator, by the presence of another

[41] We shall later refer to Eduardo Pavlovsky's 'Teatro de intensidades o de la multiplicación' (Theater of intensities or multiplication) and its impact on the 'acting poetics' of Ricardo Bartís. See the interview with Bartís in my volume *Arte y oficio del director teatral en América Latina*, dedicated to the Southern Cone.

subject. Buenaventura situates theater in a subjective dimension, which affects meaning and, for that reason, semiotics fails completely, especially if the subject is thought of—as has been done in many communicational approaches—as having full consciousness and not as a divided subject. Despite his initial enthusiasm with semiotics, Buenaventura began to consider coming gradually closer to psychoanalysis since 1969, as his talk on the actors of the TEC titled "La elaboración de los sueños y la improvisación teatral" (Dream-work and theatrical improvisation)[42] attests. In this talk, Jackobson's contributions on metaphor and metonymy intersect with those of Freud (as happens with Lacan's) in his *The Interpretation of Dreams*, and with the subject of the unconscious. If the spectacle, as signifier, is modified by the presence of the spectator, it is because something is at play in the area of demand and desire. Meaning is not a permanent condition that would admit a description by a semiotics of sign; rather it is made each time—at every show—on the relationship between the signifiers involved. And where there are signifiers the question of a divided subject must be posed. The point that needs to be addressed with Freudian structures, as Lacan has done, is to what extent the spectacle is confronted by more than one subject or to what extent, whether they know it or not, participants (*praxitioners*, audience members) have only three possible subjective positions to 'see' what is being presented: neurosis, perversion, and psychosis, on which I have based my proposal on the spectatorial structures in other essays.[43]

In his 1985 text on actor-dramaturgy, Buenaventura resorts to Julia Kristeva (whose works come from a semiotics derived from Freud and Lacan), as well as to Anne Ubersfeld. This time, the Colombian maestro will base his work on the concept of '*genotext*', a matrix "formed by a variety of texts, literary or otherwise, on which a literary text is generated". Buenaventura conceives of theatrical praxis as a *genotext*, that is, a 'representation' capable of generating a theatrical text. Every playwright writes for a given audience in attention to the conventions and subjectivity of

---

[42] In my book *Sueño. Improvisación. Teatro* (Dream. Improvisation. Theater) I have worked on Buenaventura's text in detail.

[43] See my book *Introducción a la praxis teatral. Creatividad y psicoanálisis* (Introduction to Theatrical Praxis. Creativity and Psychoanalysis).

his time, the material and technical dispositions of his environment, the actors and possible acting styles, the theater history, etc. His text prefigures the incidence of the symbolic register on the imaginary dimension. "The writer of theater—Buenaventura tells us—starts from theatrical practice in order to develop it or transform it." Thus, theatrical praxis predates the production of the dramatic text, and the latter is no more than the result of the former. The dramatic text contains the theatrical praxis from which it develops and before which it situates itself: "theatrical praxis engenders texts which in turn develop and transform it." In this way, Buenaventura tries to disarm the argument that theatrical practice is based on a dramatic text conceived of as definitive, "fixed in its form, 'to the letter', and open to interpretation in its substance, its spirit". Rather than the true consistency of theatrical practice and experience, what this conception of theatrical practice seems to manifest—says Buenaventura—is the juridical, religious, and ideological imposition of Western modernity. Later on, when the Industrial Revolution imposed the division of labor over the previous ideology, a division "between those who 'conceive' and those who 'execute'" would arise. This is a variable of the totally anti-dialectical division between intellectual and manual work, between theoretical and practical work. From this framework comes the idea of the actor-interpreter, whose creative capacity has been dimmed. For all these reasons, the staging—insists Buenaventura—cannot be conceived as a translation or an interpretation of the dramatic text. And though he does not mention it, the staging also responds to a certain matrix in the conception of direction and acting, the current aesthetics, and the technological development of theaters. The Colombian maestro quotes Ubersfeld to underscore his idea of the staging linked to the laying out of a discourse as an inevitable act for the constitution of meaning (the idea of a subject again): the staging is produced by someone for someone for a reason. However, it is not a 'sign' but a signifier for, as we have already seen, this meaning is modified by the presence of the spectator. Lacan used to say that communication is a misunderstanding. The sender's message does not get intact to the receiver, which puts the very idea of sign into question. For all these reasons—Buenaventura decidedly concludes—"the concept of dramaturgy must not be reduced to the texts written for theater." The first step in his attempt to redefine dramaturgy has been given: Buenaventura does not conceive of it as linked to the strictly verbal, to the dramatic text, the author or the literature.

From this negative characterization, Buenaventura proceeds to explore dramaturgy's consistency and in so doing he meets with action, the actor and improvisation—and, of course, with collective creation. As opposed to Pavis, Buenaventura maintains that collective creation has a long history; it is not a modern invention (least of all recent), for it goes back at least to the Commedia dell'Arte or its apogee during the sixteenth and seventeenth centuries, "*teatro all'improvviso*". Collective creation is the *geno-text* of the great Spanish Baroque, Elizabethan, and Moliere theater forms: "it is the basis, the matrix of all modern theater in the West." The Commedia dell'Arte was a theater of actors that, moreover, "established a new relationship with a new audience." However, this actor-dramaturgy will eventually fall under "the tyranny of text and that of the director, both of which will go on reducing the dramaturgic space of the actor." Consequently, Buenaventura's and the TEC's[44] proposal is not about reenacting the Commedia dell'Arte (an impossible task) rather, says he about "keeping the role of the literary text and that of the director (as well as that of the stage designer, etc.), the lost space of the actor-dramaturgy [could be] reconquered for the stage's discourse." Collective creation will thus develop as a methodology akin to the Commedia dell'Arte, though different from it.

To what extent can modern collective creation be considered actor-dramaturgy? To what extent can the practice of, for example, Eduardo Pavlovsky, be considered as modern collective creation? Are Pavlovsky's theater of multiplicity or intensity, and Bartís' actor poetics part of actor-dramaturgy? This is where categorizing problems begin, which obviously have to be discussed if we are to attain our objective of imagining a dramaturgy conceived in terms of the discourse of the Analyst.

[44] Teatro Experimental de Cali (TEC).

Buenaventura tries to 'reconquer' the space lost by the actor in the staging process, and this is what we understand as modern collective creation. The actor's ability to write onstage is retrieved at the level of staging, but not of dramatic text. He writes:

> Collective creation is often reduced to the process of elaboration of the text by actors and opposed to "author-theater". The elaboration of the text by actors, a contingent and sometimes-positive possibility, in no way defines collective creation. Moreover, the writing of the text (a task closely related to literary practice) is not, precisely, the actor's role. His dramaturgical participation lies in the writing of the spectacle's discourse at the time of staging.

Actors are rarely in charge of the final writing down of the spectacle's discourse. Usually, one of them assumes the role of director or there is an appointed director, and sometimes one of them assumes the task of writing the dramatic text or a playwright or writer is invited, which brings back the experience to that of an actor- or director-dramaturgy. Buenaventura tries to salvage creative collective as actor-dramaturgy, separating it from the experience of author and director: "With any methodology, collective creation is based on improvisation provided it is not used to prove, corroborate, improve or adorn the conception, the ideas or the staging plans of the director". Collective creation is actor-dramaturgy only at the level of the staging and only insofar as "it is accepted as the antithesis of the direction plans in the dialectic game of staging." Actor's improvisation does not define collective creation as Buenaventura conceives of it, for such improvisation may be instrumented only to illustrate or approach the author's plan, or that of the text or the director. Obviously, neither the figure of the director, nor that of the author, disappears. The director acquires here the role of mere organizer or conductor of the "score" created by the actors. In some way, creative collection, as conceived by the Colombian maestro, is nothing else but a methodological instance and, though he recognizes the creative power of the actor during the staging process, it is an actor-dramaturgy within a wider framework constituted by the director and author dramaturgy.

This framework, however, leaves unanswered the question of how the actor-dramaturgy can be perceived and appreciated in all its creativity by the spectator. In a way, both dramaturgies oppose each other dialectically during the staging process, but it is very unlikely that the final product does not respond to the director, even if he is part of the group. What differentiates modern collective creation from a regular cast formed by "interpreter" actors (that is, not creators, but those who work under the guidance of a director) is that the actors who practice it have been "trained in improvisation and [conform] a relatively stable group." This condition will be, as we shall see, determinant in an actor-dramaturgy conceived as theater of intensities. The improvisation may be even practiced in any of the dramaturgies, but it is not always creative. In order to be creative, it needs a group of actors who have been together for a given time and share certain presuppositions. In this sense, as Buenaventura states, collective creation is no better or worse than director-dramaturgy and it does not guarantee to produce better spectacles.

The Commedia dell'Arte is collective creation inasmuch as there is a stable group of actors whose creativity comes from improvisations on a given plot and with fixed types. There is no author, and the actors formulate a *script* that "wasn't the simple organization in actions of the story's plot [but rather] the conversion of the significant narrative matter into significant theatrical matter." As we have seen when discussing it as discourse of the University, modern collective creation begins with a topic and investigates it, arranges it in narrative sequences and after improvisations, when actions have been resolved, a text takes its form and its writing is allotted to an author (probably from the collective). Such text is staged under the supervision of a director who, once more, may appeal to improvisation in order to solve questions of staging, as it is done with the so-called actors-interpreters. Modern collective creation usually builds characters and, in some cases, it resorts to types, mostly taken from popular tradition. Buenaventura underscores the fact that collective creation admits to being an actor-dramaturgy provided the participating actors "do not let themselves be reduced to the condition of gifted interpreters of conceptions that in one way or another are imposed upon them," that is, as long as actors keep themselves within the margins of the discourse of the Hysteric. And this can only happen if the director decides to place himself, as we have described, in the position of Agent as $\$$ before his actors' desire. Buenaventura says this in his own words: without mentioning the "director", the Colombian maestro maintains that "The role of *direction* is no other but that of creating the conditions conducive to creation, objective conditions, that is, methodological as well as subjective, stimulating and inciting, and keeping an eye on the totality, the organicity of the structure, which escapes the actor on account of his immersion in continuity" (the italics are mine). Modern collective creation may or may not be based on an author's text or on a text that results from the collective's work, but it will be *creative* insofar as it keeps in all its vigor the "dialectic contradiction between improvisation and direction", that is, the productive contradiction between the axis "of selection or substitution, called paradigmatic, and that of continuity, called syntagmatic", the former being in charge of the director and the latter of the actors. The staging that results from it will be our little object *a* in the position of truth, as we have seen in the discourse of the Hysteric. This conception of actor-dramaturgy, as the Colombian maestro poses it, cannot occur in commercial theater, and thus he bases on this dramaturgy his hope for a renewal of national and Latin American theater.

The dramaturgy of the actor and the theater of intensities or multiplication

The theater of intensities corresponds to the actor-dramaturgy and in some aspects it may work as collective creation, but not in its modern version; there are differences that separate it from the methodology developed in Latin America from the 1970s onwards. Though it is possible to find some thought on the methods of this type of theater in the rehearsals of Argentinian Playwright Eduardo Pavlovsky, the truth is that—with or without his knowledge—other Latin American directors have approached theatrical creation in a similar (albeit less strict) form.[45] For a number of reasons we cannot describe here, but which we have studied in other publications,[46] it is not possible to affiliate Eduardo 'Tato' Pavlovsky to the Argentinian theater of his generation. His way of writing and his psychoanalytic and psychodramatic background set him apart from other playwrights, such as Griselda Gámbaro, Roberto Cossa, and Osvaldo Dragún, among others. Many of Pavlovsky's plays published today (especially those produced after his return from exile) are the result of a group-work process. His dramatic texts are a pre-text to be handed to a director for staging. His published texts are a post-text, that is, the result of the work with actors and directors very close to him and, though he signs them as "author", this authorship is not equivalent to the one we

[45] See the interviews to young directors in my volume *Arte y oficio del director teatral en América Latina* (Art and Craft of the Theater Director in Latin America).

[46] See my essays "Argentina en Cádiz: El psicoanálisis, la nueva dramaturgia y las poéticas actorales" (Argentina in Cadiz: Psychoanalysis, the new dramaturgy and acting poetics), "Improvisación y teatro de improvisación: aproximación psicoanalítica y dimensión del deseo" (Improvisation and improvisation theater: psychoanalytical approach and the dimension of desire), "Poéticas actorales, ensayo teatral y psicoanálisis: nuevo paradigma del teatro latinoamericano. Breves notas a partir de las poéticas de Eduardo Pavlovsky y Ricardo Bartís" (Acting poetics, theater rehearsal and psychoanalysis: a new paradigm of Latin American theater. Some notes on the poetics of Eduardo Pavlovsky and Ricardo Bartís), and "Antecedentes psicoanalíticos de la nueva dramaturgia argentina: Los textos 'clínicos' de Eduardo Pavlovsky" (Psychoanalytic background of the new Argentinian dramaturgy: The 'clinical' texts of Eduardo Pavlovsky).

traditionally recognize or have already described in detail in the author dramaturgy conceived as discourse of the Master. Moreover, Pavlovsky himself incites other groups to make their own proposals and explorations with his texts without close observation to what is written.

In this theater of intensities, the writing process runs parallel to the staging and the publication takes place after the premiere. In some texts there are characters, but not in all of them, as happens with other recent playwrights (Daniel Veronese in Argentina, Ana Harcha in Chile, Mariana Percovich in Uruguay, Victoria Valencia in Colombia, to name a few), whose texts sometimes appear as extensive poems that can be staged in multiple ways and with a varying number of actors. Each one of the characters, when there are more than one, proceeds from an improvisation process in which various actors have participated and are, in a certain way, multivocal. The process sets off when somebody from the group is assaulted by an image, a word or a brief story. Usually the person who carries this senseless 'clot'[47] is whom we will later know as playwright, though not necessarily. In some instances, the same person assumes the direction, though it wasn't the case with Pavlovsky.[48]

In contrast with modern collective creation, which proposed research projects in some way outside the 'subjectivity' of its members— more open themselves to an 'objective' social and political reality, which they sought to modify—the dramaturgy of the actor in the theater of intensities stems from the *fantasme*, in a psychoanalytical sense. Obviously, this *fantasme* has a relationship with the Real, in the Lacanian sense, but not a direct relationship representative of reality.

In modern collective creation the topic was linked to the explicit ideology of the group and the starting point was the idea that the topic must be investigated in order to show the conditions of production that had

[47] A way to refer to what in psychoanalysis is known as *fantasme*. The term is borrowed from Julio Cortázar.

[48] I can't resist inviting the reader to appreciate the ideological coherence of Tato Pavlovsky in this sense. In refusing to direct his texts—as other playwrights do—and keeping to the acting dimension, he refrains from monopolizing the sense as playwright and director. The staging in which he acts, though based on his text, is not proposed as *the* original version of the play but as one version among many of the director in turn. He thus maintains the openness and multiplicity inherent to his text.

been dimmed by ideology. They started from a certain position of knowledge offered to them by certain Marxist perspective. It was a theater that, without being *agit prop*, was in any case conceived as militancy (aesthetic, and/or political) and directed towards revealing the oppression and exploitation mechanisms of capitalism. The research included reading books and documents, going through victim testimonies, and inviting experts to participate on some aspect of the topic. This led to improvisation and thus the staging went on being written. The dramatic text was usually entrusted to one of the members, and sometimes a playwright was invited. As we have seen, in contrast to commercial or 'professional' theater, linked to the discourse of the Master, modern collective creation was more dependent on the discourses of the University and the Hysteric. Its objective was for the spectacle to produce a kind of knowledge capable of instructing or 'objectively' illuminating the spectator through entertainment.

The theater of intensities is about working with and from what is not known. The 'clot' may come up as a symptom or a product of the unconscious (lapse, oblivion, joke) that is, something akin to the *tyche* Lacan takes from Aristotle in *Seminar 11* in order to refer to the opening and closing dynamics characteristic of the unconscious. It is by means of this *tyche* that the Real abruptly bursts into the discourse of the ego [*moi*] altering its continuity and, obviously, taking it by surprise. The clot, for this reason, has a direct relationship with the unconscious and also with the body insofar as it involves the Real, the *jouissance*. It is not, therefore, a political or ideological a priori in the form of an idea to be developed on the stage. It is not part of militancy but of suffering; an enigma which, once the consciousness has emerged, opens up the dimension of an ethics, the ethics of psychoanalysis: once *that* has spoken, it must be acknowledged. It is no longer possible to ignore the enigma. There are no experts on this topic and the bibliography on it is limited. The clot is the result of a process that belongs to a particular actor, to his reference group. It is *one* case. And theatrical praxis operates here like psychoanalysis, on a case-by-case basis.

The theater of intensities as actor-dramaturgy cannot occur outside a tightly integrated group, for it presupposes a risk to the emotional stability of its members. Though the actors resort to improvisation, what they look forward to is not so much a staging but a way to overcome the fundamental *fantasme* that will found the spectacle. In Pavlovsky, due to his long trajectory with psychodrama, improvisation is oriented towards exploring the worst or the unrecognized in the self, that space which is rejected and even suppressed by the self. At the clinic, Pavlovsky may concern himself with the self, but in theater he is more concerned with the subject, the unconscious, even though he does not express it in those terms. As Ricardo Bartís (whose relationship with Pavlovsky is well-known) later expressed it: what matters is the biographic, on condition that it is not reduced to the personal. And when Bartís talks about the biographic he refers to what Lacan called the trans-individual unconscious, in order to differentiate it from, precisely, the collective unconscious. The trans-individual unconscious is parochial and belongs to the historical here-and-now of a group or community; it is neither universal nor archetypal or ahistorical or essential. In fact, improvisations proceed by taking things as far away as possible from comfort and towards a dimension that is negated by the self. It is a painful process. But, at the same time, the personal, the individual, the differential (as stated by J. L. Moreno, the founder of psychodrama) takes shape in a superior stratum that will have to do with the civil *fantasme* of the nation and, therefore, with what Bartís seems to define as the biographic. As an actor, Pavlovsky likes to visit with his improvisations the different characters that are delineated. Each actor explores the clot and summons his own 'forest of *fantasmes*'. As the actor passes from one character to the next, a multiplicity of voices and perspectives are produced, which Pavlovsky notes down and submits again to improvisation. Undoubtedly, this dynamic comes from psychodrama and the school of J. L. Moreno, under whom Pavlovsky studied. Let's not forget that Eduardo Pavlovsky is also the founder of the Psychodrama School in Argentina.

Interlude on psychodrama

As defined by Moreno, psychodrama "puts the patient on a stage where he can work out his problems with the aid of a few therapeutic actors" (177). It is an inter-personal therapy in which words, gestures and movements count. Under the therapist's gaze and with the help of an actor who operates as an auxiliary 'I' (a double or mirror of sorts, or an 'other' who questions him without getting to be the superego), the patient starts. Also linked to psychodrama, Boal too will take on aspects of this methodology in his Theater of the Oppressed and introduce the element of the 'joker'. We shall not go into detail here about Moreno's views on Freudian psychoanalysis and his arguments against it, but obviously psychoanalysis lies at the base of psychodrama. Not without certain pretense, Moreno claims to start from where psychoanalysis ends. Moreno's idea is to treat the patient not in the artificiality of a clinic, in isolation, but within a group facing others, not only verbally, but through actions (10, 17). Once more, some of the trans-individual seems to be under these group dynamics; without this confidence and even belief in a trans-individual unconscious, group therapy would be impossible. Moreno accuses Freud of having privileged the verbal in the 'talking cure'. This is an unjust criticism, for Freud never neglected action. In his essays on technique, and without doubt evoking his wrong handling of transference in the Dora case, Freud observes how the patient acts when she does not remember what has been forgotten and suppressed. Freud writes:

> We can say that the analysand does not *remember*, in general, a thing about the forgotten and suppressed, but that she *acts* it. She does not reproduce it as a memory but as action; she *repeats* it, not knowing, of course, that she does. (*O. C.* 12: 15-152)

As Moreno presents it, psychodrama would seem to locate itself halfway between *collective creation* and the *creative collective* mentioned by Pavis. Moreno, who traces back the origins of psychodrama to primitive rites and the Commedia dell'Arte (12,13), underlines that psychodrama is conducted within a concrete community, where expressive spontaneity and creativeness are encouraged, while dissolving both the difference between the aesthetic and the therapeutic and the difference between actors and spectators (15). Boal will attempt to do just the same with his famous spect-actor. The interesting aspect of Moreno's perspective is that in psychodrama "[c]atharsis moved from the spectator to the actor" (15) and, in a way, when he takes on the Aristotelian concept and the "cathartic method" that Freud and Breuer had experimented with and later abandoned, Moreno founds an axiom that will have important consequences for actor-dramaturgy in the future. Here, as we know, Boal does not follow Moreno, due to his aversion for and criticism of Aristotelian catharsis as a nefarious component of Western theater. Through this route, Moreno tries to take drama from the framework of imitation and bring it close to what we know today as performance art: "Psychodrama defines the drama as an extension of life and action rather than its imitation." (15)

The actor in psychodrama faces his own conflicts in the framework of a group of actors who constitute his therapeutic group. Catharsis—which Moreno classifies as somatic, mental, individual and group (16, 17)––no longer takes place among the audience (because there isn't any) or in the imaginary of a character (because there is no representation), but rather "in the spontaneous actors in the drama who produce the personae by liberating themselves from them at the same time" (Moreno 29). It is thus that group participants end up being authors, actors, and spectators. Under the supervision of a therapist who officiates as director and accompaniment, the participant 're-creates' his lived experience, as well as that which he hasn't lived in his private world. Moreno calls this director "auxiliary ego", an assistant to the group's coordinator who has been properly trained not only to adequately develop the 's factor' (spontaneity factor), but who has also explored many roles (mother, father, sister, boss, etc.) and is prepared to open up new possibilities to the conflict during the improvisations. This psychodrama-training situation shields the auxiliary ego and the actor from the risks of doing such improvisations in everyday life. During training, the subject has the possibility to freely 'rehearse' and 'experiment' new roles and give them new dimensions and even assume a different role (138) without major consequences for his private life. The training in part is close to the idea of rehearsal in traditional theater, with the difference that it shields the 's factor', that is, it keeps spontaneity alive, so that a traditional theater actor, if well trained, has the capacity to go beyond his submission to the character. Once again, we are very close to Stanislavski. Moreno states that the "great actor" has the capacity to add something new, something alive to the character created by the author in every show, even though he has represented the play a thousand times (90). In psychodrama, however, it is not about expressing the ego but about creating it: "This *s* function is not satisfied expressing only the self; it is eager to *create* the self." (91) What differentiates psychodrama and will also differentiate the theater of intensities is the act of facing the "enactable and unenactable roles" (172). Some roles are more easily recreated than others and, as happens with children, some actors find it easy to recreate those that are alien to them (such as the policeman or the taxi driver) but face difficulties when having to recreate roles that are familiar to them (father, mother, brother, etc.). It is possible to envision the difficulties Pavlovsky must have faced when working on the character of the father-torturer-children thieve in *Potestad* (Paternal authority).

The auxiliary ego identifies with the patient (author-actor-spectator) not only through words but also through actions; he co-acts with him and recreates the situation that burdens him (20). Built on the model of a maternal image who assists the child in its first months during premature motor capacity, the auxiliary ego officiates as a guide, portrays the roles and communicates them to the subject: "The natural setting of the mother-child relationship is comparable to the auxiliary ego-subject relation of the psychodramatic situation." (59) The influence of Winnicot and his transitional object is felt here, an aspect yet to be carefully developed in theatrical praxis. The actor suggests a role he needs in order to start the scene and the auxiliary ego conforms to it, but obviously with the intention of generating new possibilities for the situation.

Interestingly, Moreno maintains that the true symbol of therapeutic theater—as he often calls psychodrama—is the private home (26). It is impossible not to relate this to Freud's concept of the *Umheimlich* (uncanny, sinister, ominous).[49] For Freud, the uncanny is what produces anxiety because it is both familiar (*Heimlich*) and unfamiliar, an alien that comes back, not necessarily unknown. This concept is also related to the topic of the double (patient and auxiliary ego). Clearly, the theater of intensities as actor-dramaturgy situates its field of exploration in relation to a familiar field (the private, the neighborhood, the national) and explores the way in which the uncanny is located in everyday dynamics. Moreno acknowledges that from childhood—to which he dedicates extensive studies—every individual is modeled by the symbolic: he 'acts' in everyday life by reproducing a series of roles and conceives of it with certain degree of theatricality. When talking about sociodrama, Moreno insists, "[e]very role is a fusion of private and collective elements." (62, note 4) However, the roles acted in life and the roles acted onstage have little in common, and undoubtedly their meanings are different (35). In everyday life, "we are far more acted upon than acting" (35-36), that is, we are acted, spoken by the Other or, as Moreno says, we are creatures in everyday life, but in scenic fiction we are creators, which obviously we have to take with reservations. However, the idea of seeing oneself in the other, in the auxiliary ego, or seeing oneself through the relations proposed by the other members of the group generates a *distance* that allows not only to lucubrate new possibilities for the conflict that afflicts us but also to approach it by transforming the effective suffering of everyday life (to which Moreno calls "real") in laughter, thus making it more bearable, more liberating (29). Because it is based on spontaneity, the play with the auxiliary ego and other participants opens up possibilities for the emergence of surprise, the unexpected (35). Spontaneous creativity breaks the causal chain of everyday life and presents it as less limiting. It is interesting that, despite Moreno's efforts to set himself apart from Stanislavsky (38-39), he resorts to the famous "as if": on the stage, the participant acts as if he were in

[49] See S. Freud's "The Uncanny" in the *Standard Edition of the Complete Psychological Works*, Vol. XVII (1917-1919).

everyday life, though no longer responding to a causal sequence ("I have a toothache, so I call the dentist"), but using all the elements (telephone, dentist, impulses, etc.) as "materials of a strategy for a fictitious purpose." (35) Moreno tries to differentiate himself from Stanislavsky and Freud because, according to him, both the Russian and the Austrian maestros are preoccupied with an earlier text from the past, a suppressed one which resides in the unconscious and is the seat of the subject's childhood experiences, the most intensive ones. In a little of a contradiction with some of his earlier affirmations on the way in which the symbolic imposes certain roles with defined strict protocols, Moreno thinks that the psychodrama actor develops his role "*in statu nascendi*" (39), spontaneously. He tries in this way to underscore the idea of the moment, the present, which is necessary for his theory of spontaneity. But psychodrama has a kinship with the happening and with performance art: "the act of creation is contemporaneous with the production" (41). Moreno calls it "Impromptu performance" (41) thus revealing the influence of what we know as theater of improvisation (match for the improvisation).[50] The audience, says Moreno, functions as though they were a thousand dramaturges (1). In the same way, obviously, the group in which the patient participates acts as a group, and thus writes.

[50] See my essay "Improvisación y teatro de improvisación: aproximación psicoanalítica y dimensión del deseo" (Improvisation and theater of improvisation: psychoanalytical approach and the dimension of desire).

Theater of intensity or multiplication

What we must retain here is that, though starting from the personal, the actors slowly progress into a dimension that is, so to speak, above them: the biographical, as we have seen, is a network of confluences in which the imaginary intersects with the symbolic after having stumbled with the solid rock of the real, not reality. The Real is that which lacks signifier. It is often the case that the biographic—and consequently the *fantasme*, what I have at some point defined as the civil *fantasme* of the nation that unites a group—is, as the trans-individual unconscious, a secret channel of suppressed or denied communications, which brings one group together for reasons of age or generation, common experiences, shared suffering and longings; in short, a shared memory. The participants improvise in the dimension of the not knowing; they have no way of ensconcing in the realm of the known or accepted. Thus, in *El Señor Galíndez* and *Potestad*, Pavlovsky explores the *fantasme* of the torturer and, as we shall see, on this same track he is going to address a spectator, not to illuminate him about what he ignores, but to involve him—and inconvenience him from another ethics—in the horror of civil complicity with torture, be it the one exercised by the State, or paramilitary groups, the superego or the role that each member of the audience exercises in their own family and everyday life. The spectator who is seated watching the spectacles of the theater of the intensity cannot avoid seeing himself onstage, seeing there what he doesn't want to see in himself and his everyday life. Let's remember that, for Lacan, the *fantasme* is a scene in which the subject sees himself and, at the same time, from which he is included. In Pavlovsky, as in other dramaturges of his generation, it is not about presenting a scenic theorem in which there are "good" and "bad" people––sometimes totally good or bad—and in which the story, with more or less effort, ends up with the triumph of the good. It is neither about thinking that the 'others' are the evil ones and that the spectator, knowing it or not, feels he is 'good' and above—or even stranger—to that atrocity. Pavlovsky's spectacles are disturbing because they force the spectator to process part of his guilt, his involvement and responsibility with what it is being developed onstage. As in *Potestad*, a good father may be *at the same time* a torturer; a torturer is not necessarily deprived of fatherly tenderness. Any father in the audience has to elaborate his uncanny side, which probably slips even in the splendor of his deepest tenderness. In *El Señor Galíndez*, a boy full of life and sympathy can be a sorcerer's apprentice, a harmless cleaning lady may be an accomplice to the most terrible atrocities, and conversely, some women of the street may turn into victims of something more devastating than their profession: the experimental excesses of power. In Pavlovsky it is not about a scene with white and black undertones in which the spectator can reinforce his identification with what he sees as long as he feels separated from it and, in that way, feel redeemed from his silent complicity before a reality that, notwithstanding, is not so far from the stage. Moreover, it is not about each member of the audience purifying through catharsis their passions, complicity, and guilt so that they come out of the theater pacified with the horror and the Real. The idea is for each member of the audience to elaborate the way of *jouissance* in which they are captured and the actions to which they are taken by such capture of the *jouissance* of the Other in the hegemonic discourse.

Since the interest of the theater of intensity lies in the Real and not in reality, it is understandable that its discourse be sometimes a little cryptic for the common spectator and have no aim to instruct or illuminate the audience. It is not, however, a cryptic text but a ciphered one, which all members of the audience are invited to decipher from their own singular subjectivity, so that working on their mode of *jouissance* they manage to emancipate themselves from the *jouissance* of the hegemonic Other[51] and, in this way, proceed ethically in relation to their desire and politically in the democratic debate from an emancipated desire and *jouissance*.

[51] I use the word 'emancipation' to differentiate analytic work from the liberationist discourses of past decades and still partially ongoing. See my essay "Una reflexión sobre las nociones de 'liberación' y 'emancipación'. Su pertinencia en la praxis teatral" (A reflection on the notions of 'liberation' and 'emancipation'. Their relevance to theatrical praxis).

It is understandable that the signifiers on the stage not always have the 'clarity' of a 'well-structured' argument from a supposedly pure rationality. The theater of intensities and theatrical praxis are characterized by their distancing from the narrative premises of Aristotelian tradition. In the theater of Victoria Valencia (for example, *Rubiela roja*[52]) the characters go through the recesses of their most desperate existential experiences, immersed as they are in a crossroads of death and marginalities, and they attain, by way of a poetry of atrocious extravagance, the *fantasme* of *violence* in a dimension that modern collective creation could never attain. The participants in this kind of dramaturgy do not place themselves above the public as vehicles of a *savoir* that the others lack. They simply share their biographical upheavals (not personal), which means that they offer the audience the scene of the civil *fantasme* just at it encroaches in the everyday life of a community and their trans-individual unconscious. In my theatrical praxis, these procedures resulted in *Las mujeres de Juárez del Mundo* (The World's Women of Juarez), where we didn't postulate any knowledge of the murders of Ciudad Juarez (who really happened to know?) but rather approached those dead women in our bodies, in our way of *jouissance* and in our complicity with the subjugation of desire in neoliberal society. In a way, beyond theorizing over the *fantasme*, as Lacan would later do, there is certain influence of psychodrama here insofar as, in J. L. Moreno's words, "[t]he individual is urged to face the truth that these experiences are not really 'his', but public psychological property" (11). The spectator in this kind of theater of intensity—whether he responds or not to the procedures of a post-dramatic theater already described—does not take away 'a meaning' of the spectacle but a demand for meaning, a half-saying of the truth which is the only way that the spectator will gradually ponder over his own desire at the end of the show. Frustrated in his demand of totality of meaning, the spectator—as did the actor before him—sees himself confronted by the spectacle, which now occupies the posi-

[52] Featured in *Antología del teatro latinoamericano (1950-2007)* (An Anthology of Latin American Theater, 1950-2007) compiled by Lola Proaño and Gustavo Geirola.

tion of Agent as object *a*. The spectacle has also responded him with enigmas rather than formulas for a guaranteed collective well-being, promises of adaptation to an ethics or a value supposedly universal, or utopias or difficult realization.

Is it then possible to think of the theater of intensities as a dramaturgy of the actor conceived as the discourse of the Analyst? All seems to indicate that it is indeed, provided that the subject that occupies the position of the Agent does it as *a*, that is, he does not occupy the place of truth, or that of the Master, or that of the University. The minimum attempt to direct the content of improvisations towards a specific thesis, the minimum gesture of wanting to give 'coherence' and totality to the spectacle, the slightest intention to seduce the actors and take them to an identification with an ideal or satisfy their entire demand for *savoir* would suffice to immediately turn this actor-dramaturgy from theater of the intensity into modern collective creation or traditional theater. The director may function as counterpart (or countenance[53]) of *a*, provided he does not really believe he is the *a* of his actors. He must not always respond as though he could say the 'whole' truth of what goes on in the rehearsals or on the stage. In this dramaturgy, the actor has to keep—as we have already said for the spectator—the unsatisfied demand, for it is this demand which will stimulate him to keep his creativity and his desire alive onstage, during the show and through the season, insofar as it will incite him to continue working on what he discovers throughout the process, the signifiers that continue to appear. Clearly, this dramaturgy is not made for commercial circuits; there is no space here for punctuated and unchanging scenic directions, nor can a Stanislavskian-style[54] actor-machine fulfill an already established program: a space of uncertainty must exist here so that the unconscious, with its pulsating characteristic, can speak; there must be a space here for the signifier—and not only verbal—to stumble and thus reopen the work of creativity. Finally, there must be a space in which transference can install itself.

---

[53] The French *semblable* used by Lacan has been translated into Spanish as *semblante*. Evans, in his Lacanian Dictionary, translates it as "counterpart", which does not seem to capture the Lacanian meaning attributed to that very important psychoanalytical term.

[54] See my essay "Los cuerpos del actor" (The actor's bodies).

BIBLIOGRAPHY

Barba, Eugenio. "Un amuleto hecho de memoria. El significado de los ejercicios en la dramaturgia del actor". http://www10.ocn.ne.jp/~kunstart/barba_espanol.htm

Borgna, Gabriela. "Escribir en un espacio y un cuerpo emocionados", en *Revista Picadero*, año 2, nº 7, Buenos Aires: Instituto Nacional del Teatro, 2002, pp. 23-25. Citado por María Fernanda Pinta en "Dramaturgia del actor y técnicas de improvisación. Escrituras teatrales contemporáneas".

Buenaventura, Enrique. "La elaboración de los Sueños y la Improvisación Teatral". Buenaventura, Enrique y Jacqueline Vidal. *Esquema General del Método de Trabajo Colectivo del Teatro Experimental de Cali y otros ensayos.* Maracaibo: Universidad de Zulia, 2005. 55-65

---. "La dramaturgia de actor".1985 http://www.teatrodelpueblo.org.ar/dramaturgia/buenaventura001.htm

Freud, Sigmund. *Obras Completas.* Buenos Aires: Editorial Amorrortu, fechas diversas.

Geirola, Gustavo. *Introducción a la praxis teatral. Creatividad y psicoanálisis* (Introduction to Theatrical Praxis. Creativity and Psychoanalysis). Buenos Aires/Los Ángeles: Argus-*a*, 2022.

Arte y oficio del director teatral en América Latina. 6 volúmenes. Buenos Aires/ Los Ángeles: Argus-*a* Artes y Humanidades/Arts and Humanities, varios años.

---. "Interpretando el adjetivo 'áfono' en relación a la voz como objeto a". Argus-*a* Artes y Humanidades/Arts & Humanities XII.45 (Septiembre 2022)

---. "Una reflexión sobre las nociones de 'liberación' y 'emancipación'. Su pertinencia en la praxis teatral". Stephan Arnulf Baumgartel Luiz Gustavo Bieberbach Engro, José Ricardo Goulart [ORGS.]. *Ensaiando o olhar latino-americano: insistência de uma cena situada.* Rio de Janeiro: Mórula, 2021.

---. "Patriarcado, crimen y sociedad postedípica en dos obras de Hugo Salcedo: Hacia un teatro de emancipación". Argus-*a* Artes y Humanidades/Arts & Humanities IX.36 (June 2020).

https://www.argus-a.com/publicacion/1477-patriarcado-crimen-y-sociedad-postedipica-en-dos-obras-de-hugo-salcedo-hacia-un-teatro-de-emancipacion.html

---. *Sueño. Improvisación. Teatro. Ensayos sobre la praxis teatral.* Buenos Aires/Los Ángeles: Argus-*a* Artes y Humanidades/Arts & Humanities, 2019.

---. "La praxis teatral y lo político: la demanda, el teatrista, el público". *Revista telondefondo* (29 (2019). http://revistascientificas.filo.uba.ar/index.php/telondefondo/article/view/6510

---. "Justicia, neoliberalismo y extimidad: A propósito de *Hambre*, de Merly Macías". Argus-*a* Artes y Humanidades/Arts & Humanities VIII. 30 (Dec 2018). http://www.argus-a.com.ar/archivos-dinamicas/1382-1.pdf

---. *¡Todo a pulmón! Entrevistas a diez teatristas argentinos.* Co-editado con Lola Proaño. Buenos Aires/Los Angeles: Argus-*a* Artes y Humanidades/Arts & Humanities, 2016.

---. "Los cuerpos del actor." Encinas, Percy, ed. *Stanislavski desde nuestros teatros. Recreación de su legado.* Lima: AIBAL/PUCP, 2015. 29 – 54 http://gustavogeirolaensayos.blogspot.com/

---. Praxis teatral y puesta en escena: la psicosis como máscara espectatorial en el ensayo teatral (1ra. Parte). *Telondefondo* Revista de teoría y crítica teatral 9.18 (2013).

---. Praxis teatral y puesta en escena: la psicosis como máscara espectatorial en el ensayo teatral (1ra. Parte). *Telondefondo* Revista de teoría y crítica teatral 9.17 (2013).

---. "El director y su público: la puesta en escena y las estructuras espectatoriales." *Telondefondo* Revista de teoría y crítica teatral 8.15 (2012).

---. *Antología de teatro latinoamericano (1950-2007).* Co-editor with Lola Proaño-Gómez.Buenos Aires: Instituto Nacional de Teatro, 2010.

---. "Aproximación lacaniana a la teatralidad del teatro: desde la fase del espejo al modelo óptico. Notas para interrogar nuestras ideas cotidianas sobre el teatro y el realismo". Pelletieri, Osvaldo, ed. *En torno a la convención y la novedad.* Buenos Aires: Galerna/Fundación Roberto Arlt, 2009. 33-52.

---. "Improvisación y teatro de improvisación: aproximación psicoanalítica y dimensión del deseo", en *Perpectivas teatrales*, Os-valdo Pellettieri (ed.), Buenos Aires: Galerna, 2008. 25-49.

---. "La creación colectiva y el teatro creativo en la perspectiva de Platon-Michailovic Keržencev y la Revolución Rusa". *Dramateatro Revista Digital*, Septiembre 2008, Caracas, Venezuela.

---. "Antecedentes psicoanalíticos de la nueva dramaturgia argentina: Los textos "clínicos" de Eduardo Pavlovsky". *Revista telondefondo* 4.8 (Diciembre 2008). http://www.telondefondo.org/home.php

---. "Improvisación y teatro de improvisación: aproximación psicoanalítica y dimensión del deseo", en *Perpectivas teatrales*, Osvaldo Pellettieri (ed.), Buenos Aires: Galerna, 2008. 25-49.

---. "Poéticas actorales, ensayo teatral y psicoanálisis: nuevo paradigma del teatro latinoamericano. Breves notas a partir de las poéticas de Eduardo Pavlovsky y Ricardo Bartís." *ATeatro* 12 (2007): 78-87.

---. "Argentina en Cádiz: El psicoanálisis, la nueva dramaturgia y las poéticas actorales." Rizk, Beatriz y Luis Ramos-García, eds. *Panorama de las artes escénicas ibérico y latinoamericanas: Homenaje al Festival Iberoamericano de Cádiz.* Minneapolis-Cadiz: University of Minnesota and Patronato del FIT de Cadiz, 2007. 55-82

---. *Teatralidad y experiencia política en América Latina.* 1ra. Edición: California: Ediciones de Gestos, 2000. 2da. Edición: Argus-*a* Artes y Huma-nidades/Arts & Humanities, 2018.

Lacan, Jacques. *Seminario 18 De un discurso que no fuera semblante.* Buenos Aires: Paidós, 2009.

---. *Seminario 10 La angustia.* Buenos Aires: Paidós, 2006.

---. *Seminario 11 Los cuatro conceptos fundamentales del psicoanálisis.* Buenos Aires: Paidós, 1987.

---. *Escritos.* Buenos Aires: Siglo XXI Editores, 2002.

---. *Seminario 17 El reverso del psicoanálisis.* Buenos Aires: Paidós, 1996.

---. *Seminario 20 Aun.* Buenos Aires: Paidós, 1985.

---. *Psicoanálisis. Radiofonía y Televisión*. Barcelona: Anagrama, 1977.

Malcún, Juan Carlos. *Espacio escénico. Texto, contexto y sentido*. Buenos Aires: Editorial Nueva Generación, 2020.

Moreno, J. L. *Psicodrama*. New York: Beacon House, 1946.

Pavis, Patrice. *Dictionary of the Theatre*. Toronto and Buffalo: University of Toronto Press, 1998.

Saussure, Ferdinand de. *Curso de Lingüística General*. Buenos Aires: Editorial Losada, 1945.

Addendum

Collective creation and creative theater from the perspective of Platon Michailovic Keržencev and the Russian Revolution

Platon Michailovic Keržencev (1881-1940) had an important participation in government bodies before and after the Revolution of 1917, especially those dedicated to culture and particularly the arts and theater. His project, transformed through the years as the Revolution progressed and the Party consolidated its power, can be read in his communications at different conferences as well as reports to specific committees, especially in his book *Creative Theater: Proletarian Theater in the 1920s in Russia*, published for the first time in 1918 and followed by several versions and successive editions until the fifth edition of 1923.

The book presents itself—says Cruziani in the Introduction—not as a theory but as a manual for cultural agents whose task is to organize the "new theater". Throughout its five editions, the book constitutes a reflection that widens the project through discussions and from everyday practice (xi-xii). Obviously, Keržencev reacts against bourgeois theater, declamation, the theater conceived by a few for a privileged many and—in clear allusion to commercial theater—against theater as exchange value, the objective of which is monetary gain. Keržencev's project must be understood in the context of post-revolutionary Russia, the Russia of transition from a bourgeois to a classless society in which theaters proliferate along with the euphoria for radical renovation. We must also understand his controversy with some revolutionary leaders (Lenin Trotsky, Lunacharsky) and some renowned artists (Meyerhold) in the process of institutionalization of the Revolution, which took place after the first years of its outbreak. This is too complex a process to be dealt with here.

Rudinsky and Robert Leach offer and interesting panorama of theater at the time of the Russian Revolution. In general terms, this is a stage in which euphoria could give way to cultural anarchy, a moment in which extreme-left radical positions intermingle with reformist ones—bourgeois residues not wholly eliminated—and in which the Party begins to identify what in its opinion configures the wrong sense of the Revolution. Both the Proletkult[55] and Keržencev have to face this euphoria in which professionals, amateurs, and people with no theatrical formation whatsoever get together to make theater. Theatrical activity, formerly reserved in some way for a few—Stanislavsky's Moscow Art Theater, for example—is now a possible medium of collective expression, wide enough as to include several discourses and perspectives.[56] In this context of cultural and ideological buoyance, the sending subject is collectivized and gets confused or coexists with the receiving subject. Clearly, no revolution is going to allow for long such indiscriminate access to the word, and its consequent institutionalization will impose administrative control processes as well as precise instructions to direct the activity through supposedly revolutionary lanes. Revolutionary or not, any discursive excess threatens social cohesion and sooner or later becomes an object of censorship, repression, and persecution.

Keržencev's dream is to open a space for collective creativity and make its expression accessible to all. It is the realization of theater as use value. He then goes on to start a crusade that is not only artistic but also political, and from it he criticizes not so much bourgeois theater as a product (drama, spectacle) but essentially theater's bourgeois means of production. For him, theater is an element of popular instruction, an active and creative force, and therefore biomechanics, with its technical, musical and gymnastical base, should not be restricted to theater but encompass social life in its entirety, especially the work life of the young in the factory (xxii). Keržencev opposes the idea of speeding up the process of formation of a proletarian culture in a society in transition. In general terms, he endorses (though not radically) the iconoclastic project that called for the complete disappearance of pre-Revolution theater. He proposes the nationalization of existing theater and its affiliation to proletarian companies; moreover, he proposes that professionals be sent to the provinces and calls for the formation of a new repertoire and of non-professional

[55] Proletarian culture, a term coined to designate the institution in charge of artistic affairs at the time [Translator's note].

[56] Cruciani offers a classification of theatrical activity in 1923 in the following way: 34% corresponded to the collective property of actors; 21% to the unions, the Red Army, and other public organizations, and 36% to the State (xix).

companies (xiv). Keržencev favors (though cautiously) the autonomy of the Proletkult as long as its radical and iconoclastic positions do not influence the revolutionary political direction. He thus opens a space of experimentation, from which he trusts will emerge the directives for a proletarian and popular theater. Keržencev has, in this sense, a rather instrumentalist or even utilitarian vision of theater, which for him is not so much an art product as it is an instrument of creativity embedded in the concreteness of everyday life.

Keržencev believes that the separation between theater and life, the stage and the spectator, must be abolished and overcome in both aesthetic and architectural terms. He thinks of an enormous scenic space capable of housing large groups and carrying out a synthesis (more intellectual than architectural) of circus and theater (87) or, even better, the Japanese design (88). With great intuition, Keržencev observes what I have elsewhere called the politics of gaze in the construction of theatricality (Geirola 2000). Architectural design—says Keržencev with great lucidity—reproduces class struggle, and a new political optics that not only promotes a new dramaturgy but also creates a new spatial design is urgently needed (49). A look at the Italian-style theater hall would suffice to immediately confirm that the total vision of the stage is only reserved to the royal or government box (the real eye) from which stage designers plan their perspective. As soon as the spectator moves above or below this box or to one side or the other, something of the stage is lost to him. Since those spaces have a varying price depending on their visibility, the Italian-style design, derived from the European aristocracy and then consecrated by the bourgeoisie, reproduces to the letter the capitalist rule of "what you see is what you pay for". We know that this aspect was intensely debated in those transition years and widely experimented by several groups and artists of the stature of Meyerhold.

Collective creation and *improvisation* were the crucial points of this project at the operational level. Keržencev himself presented in 1919 a proposal to favor collective theater and promote the formation of a hitherto inexistent repertoire (78) by way of collective improvisation. His ideas (some of them based on Romain Rolland's *The People's Theater*) will have an immediate projection on the Russian theater of the time and on the theater of every proletarian revolutionary process thereafter. In this sense, it is important to consider his proposals in detail and compare them to what in Latin America has been called *collective creation*. Keržencev is convinced that collective creation is the right cultural space for the "dramatic instinct" of the proletariat to emerge, one that will be able to collectivize the various roles that are part of the theatrical creativity process at the levels of dramaturgical production and staging (50). Three requisites define theatrical collective work: turning collective interests into staging, organizing work so as to exclude authoritarianism and open a wide space for criticism, and finally, the commitment of each participant in achieving these objectives (90).

Keržencev does not ignore the difficulties of a theater of collective creation at a revolutionary transitional stage. To begin with, controversies are expressed about avant-garde movements such as futurism, which question bourgeois drama but which do not make a revolutionary contribution from a Marxist perspective. Secondly, it is necessary to confront the practice of professionals and academics (such as those of the Moscow Art Theater) who obviously resist lowering their standards and abilities to the level of non-professionals. Thirdly, the need to review the classical repertoire adds to the problem of the inexistence of a useful dramaturgy and repertoire. But, above all, Keržencev is concerned about the lack of a new system of production, a revolutionary actor's profile, an adequate reading of popular tradition, and of concrete spaces to carry out the collective and proletarian theatrical event according to its new aesthetic standards. These questions, excessively tense as the centralist party and government demands proceed, will configure the framework in which the theatrical and aesthetic debates by Meyerhold, Eisenstein and many others (including of course Keržencev's preoccupations) must be located.

In this context, proposals are rapidly being presented and rectified, not without opening new horizons and acrid critical debates that were plagued with contradictions. Keržencev is convinced—it is almost his fundamental thesis—that theater won't be transformed by simply applying an acting technique or style, and that to achieve such transformation a radical change of the entire system of production is necessary. In this sense, he is going to attack all reformist projects in the areas of architecture, dramaturgy, and staging. In Keržencev's times, as in the present, contradictions abounded between creativity and organization, spontaneity and calculus, centralization and decentralization, autonomy and control.

The unresolved aspects at the aesthetic and political-administrative levels have continued to the present, especially at the moment of addressing the methodology of collective creation in Latin American theater. As is widely known, this methodology begins to undergo transformation at the end of the 1950s, and its role will be fundamental after the Cuban Revolution. Their protagonists, especially participants of the TEC, of Teatro de la Candelaria, of the Libre Teatro Libre, of Teatro del Escambray, with their respective directors Enrique Buenaventura, Santiago García, María Escudero and Albio Paz, put up an enormous effort to overcome the level of recipe-book or manual in order to configure a technique, a methodology, and even a theory of collective creation. It will at some point be necessary and convenient to go back to this debate and evaluate its achievements and failures, as well as the transformations they effected. Current Latin American dramaturgy has considerably benefited from collective creation, though the latter has lost steam in other approaches to theater staging and writing as, for example, in the dramaturgy of the actor. In view of the decline of 'classical' collective creation, it would be important to conduct an evaluation of its real contribution to the theater of the region.

Keržencev's basic distinction between theater *of* the people and theater *for* the people is also present in Romain Rolland and many Latin American praxitioners, including Boal in his Theater of the Oppressed. From Rolland comes the idea of a theater and a creative theatrical energy that encompasses the whole social sphere: the idea is for the people to elaborate their own revolutionary epic poem through a very dynamic theater that transcends the walls of a theater hall to take to the streets, squares, and markets in what constitutes almost a festivity. From this it is possible to discern what we would today call 'artivism', as in street protests whose performativity can take on a festive tone. For Keržencev, this is not about creating a popular theater understood as theater *for* the people, by giving workers access to the Moscow Theater or annulling the difference between stage and box, or reducing the entrance fee, but about promoting a theater *of* the people, that is, establishing the bases for the people to make their own theater, express their preoccupations and dreams, and turn into agents of their own aesthetics (35). In this sense, the author anticipates what today we call "community theater", which in many countries, notably Argentina, has a considerable development. Again, the question is not to reform theater by producing spectacles for a "popular audience" (Keržencev's own quotes) but to revolutionize theater, giving people the means of production so that they can make their own. As Cruciani tells us, Keržencev sees the club and theater school as the bases for the new theater, a civilizing and centripetal cell of which theater is the most socializing and pedagogical moment (xxiii): in the new society, says Keržencev, theater is going to configure an element of education and mass formation, as would occur in bourgeois society with the school and the university (158).

This is why, at the beginning of his *Creative Theater*, Keržencev identifies the main points of controversy, which, undoubtedly, are the ones that reappeared in Latin America at the beginning of the 1960s: the participation of the spectators, improvisation, the open-space mass spectacle and collective creation (3). A review of the Latin American proposals of collective creation can easily show the difficulties arising in, for example, trying to theorize about participation: not the Brechtian-style critical position of the spectator but his conversion from spectator to participant, with all the political consequences it entails and the social dynamics it opens up (51). Keržencev insists that his project is not limited to promoting that the spectator "recite with" the actor, sing next to the stage or close the spectacle with a feast or by singing *The Internationale*, as happened in Russia at that time and still happens today. It is about collectivizing theatrical production, making the spectator to become co-author of the spectacle (53). This aspect, so crucial for the Russia of the time or for the Cuban Revolution, so closely linked to the acrid debates arising from audience research—be it reflexology or behaviorism—remains unsolved today and, as far as I can tell, no theoretical effort to address this has yet been made.

As we know, the participation and role of the audience as co-author was a very precise preoccupation of many Latin-American groups. Santiago García, for example, discusses this aspect in great detail in his book *Teoría y práctica del teatro* (Theater's Theory and Practice). However, the concept of theory many Latin American praxitioners have (Santiago García and Enrique Buenaventura, for example) does not go beyond a modeling of theatrical practice through some structuralist schemes coming from the linguistics or semiotics of the 1960s and 1970s. This modeling, which somehow accommodates experiences that are difficult to describe, is obviously very far from being theory in a strict or dialectical and productive sense. The model is applicable, but a theory is a field of abstract concepts that operate in a context of discovery. A theory is what supports praxis, which, in principle, is inapplicable. Maybe today we would have to start, more than from a given orthodoxy of collective creation, from Enrique Buenaventura, especially from an early talk offered to the actors of the TEC in 1969 on "The elaboration of dreams and theatrical improvisation". There is a field of questions there, which go beyond formal linguistics. In fact, when introducing psychoanalysis and theorizing from the level of the unconscious and its relevance to theatrical praxis, Buenaventura finds himself in need for a less conjectural and modelizing conceptual tool, for example, the signifier, metaphor, and metonymy, as theorized by Lacan. A new dramaturgic horizon was foreseen there, which, had it continued, it would have led to the articulation of key concepts such as the *fantasme*, the temporality of the theatrical rehearsal, desire and demand, *jouissance*, transference, etc. Not by chance have these concepts been developed in Argentinian dramaturgy, with Buenos Aires as the Latin American capital of psychoanalysis (Geirola 2006, 2007b, 2008). It will suffice to approach the dramaturgy of Eduardo Pavlovsky and Ricardo Bartís to appreciate the emergence of a theatrical work dynamics that greatly differs from collective creation in its proposals and theoretical tradition.[57]

Keržencev reviews the theatrical activity of that post-revolutionary moment and finds that there is a great revival of cabaret in the small theaters of the European capitals, as well as a glorification, almost religious, of the music hall in large US cities (9). With their constant appeal to the audience and their dynamic conversation, cabaret and camera-theater have somehow eliminated the barrier between the stage and the spectator, and with their cannibalism of the social crisis they have achieved a certain critique of capitalist life. But to the eyes of Keržencev, both are limited to the merely technical and continue to be a theater of minorities involved in the entertainment of a few (32). A look at the state of modern European theater shows a lack of a repertoire and a virtual absence of dramaturges, especially those interested in a theater that goes beyond pleasing the bourgeoisie and amassing fame and money. Worse even, the representation of a drama piece follows a fixed and precise model everywhere, with an ever more marked separation between actor and spectator and a greater insistence on the passivity of the audience. However, Keržencev thinks that an old repertoire represented by a workers' company to an audience composed of workers would undoubtedly adopt a new aspect (77).

Keržencev compares the theatrical and drama production of bourgeois capitalist Europe with that of Japanese theater, which, in his opinion, has not been superseded in many aspects. He feels attracted to the use of music and rhythm that prepare the dramatic action and calibrate the actors' movement. Similarly, he feels attracted by the presence in puppet theater and in Japanese theater of invisible actors who, dressed in black, manipulate the puppets and change the scenography (21). According to Keržencev, dance goes back to the oldest roots of theatrical expression, and so it occupies a privileged place in popular theater. The bourgeoisie, says he, has divided the arts and promoted breaks and isolation, specialization and dispersion in their midst, but the new revolutionary era opens up the possibility of unifying creatively the several art genres in theatrical representation (23).

[57] See, for example, the "Interview to Ricardo Bartís" in Geirola 2007a. 125-145.

As for the relations between theater and literature, Keržencev maintains that both are closely intermingled. While the art of speech has points of contact with painting, music and other artistic genres, theater can simply not exist without literature. Though in pantomime the word is absent, the theme is linked to literature (22). From modern European drama, Keržencev rejects the way it represents the cruel destiny that turns human experience into that of vanity, as well as the cult to the mystical, the unknown, and the irrational.

However, his project will soon meet with problems. What will be the organizing form of a proletarian theater? How will future actors be trained? How will access to collective creation and the emergence of a new repertoire be promoted? How to reconsider past theatrical traditions? How to establish an organic relationship between proletarian theater and peasant theater? How to make theater in a society still divided by class? How to propose a new theater to an audience not yet homogenous and composed by all social strata and with a wide range of world-views? (48). In bourgeois theater there is usually an entrepreneur or the State is present, which, contrary to general belief, curtails the artistic freedom of praxitioners and imposes their repertoires as well as their working conditions (169). Moreover, bourgeois artists, even those who have a popular orientation and are preoccupied by the decadence of capitalism and the transition to the new society, think—in their ingrained individualism—of the new theater as a religious, medieval theater. However, in contrast with the missionary orientation of some Latin American praxitioners of the 1960s, who submitted aesthetics to religion, Keržencev thinks that the collective celebration that eliminates the separation between actor and spectator should not be submitted to the religious factor, far as it is from the future proletarian theater (49).

Keržencev proposes several routes of action and stages to attain the objectives of a proletarian theater. On the one hand, there is the need for a nationalization of bourgeois theater, that is, the transition from national-scale theater to centralized power; on the other hand, the organization of theater administration at the municipal level by the local Soviet (160). It is important to underline that Keržencev does not think this can be made in one day. He is convinced that proletarian theater will emerge insofar as "neighborhood theater" and "district theater" are fostered along with theater at the workplace, especially in factories (56). This, he maintains, would set the basis of a real unity between theater and the masses (57). This theatrical activity would require no specialized theater halls, as the groups would present their work in the street and the square (63). Theater is not conceived of as an additional task, dependent on another one deemed more important or essential. On the contrary, for Keržencev theater must remain as a perennial laboratory in which people can learn and acquire useful lifelong abilities in an environment characterized by energy and enthusiasm, where everyday there is a premiere and there are no principal and secondary roles (58, 60). Theater would thus be presented as something accessible to all and, more importantly, not necessarily a spectacle but an arena for theatrical creativity (59). This is why, apart from sending professional actors to the provinces and marginal neighborhoods, once the stage of nationalization is reached, support by aficionados will also be required.

The role of aficionados in the theater of transition was widely discussed. Many proposed its total cancellation in the construction of a proletarian theater, but Keržencev believed it necessary to safeguard their contribution (58) for, as has been already seen in the case of bourgeois theater, aficionados constituted and still constitute an alternative for renewal in the new society. The specialization of workers in the field of art, their professionalization, is something that will be achieved at the more advanced stages of the process. However, this must not be regarded as a task to train "good actors" but rather as something related to the collective production of a socialist repertoire (60). These actors can never lose contact with the working masses (66). The objective of a proletarian theater school is to devise its own techniques and provide the worker with the necessary tools to develop his own product (71). A historical evaluation of the achievements of the Soviet efforts and of the way their postulates were applied by the left in Latin American countries is yet to be done. As we now, while many of Keržencev's early theses had an energizing effect on the Soviet theatrical scene, others were never realized, ended up in a huge bureaucratic apparatus and state control, or failed completely.

Dramaturgy is a very complicated thing in a society in transition to socialism. What to represent, and in what way? How are the new plays and their staging going to look like? Keržencev goes through many of these questions, as did many Latin American artists in the 1960s and 1970s. Starting from Romain Rolland, Keržencev suggests at times the promotion of popular festivities and historical drama (65), which are always accompanied by musical grandiloquence, and he shows interest in the great massive Russian spectacles of the time. He defines popular festivity as the joyful, euphoric collective participation of the masses, with no class distinctions (110). Inasmuch as they are a real struggle against religion (117), these festivities are stimulating acts that bring energy to the masses and, for that reason, Keržencev—once again with his instrumentalist-utilitarian strategy—deems them indispensable to involve workers in their organization and promote their enthusiasm for the arts (theater, dance, singing). He also insists that it is not about getting young workers to act new plays and themes in the old format. The task is a harder and more difficult one: it is about introducing a new theatrical work system pointing towards a new representation and a new dramaturgy. The artistic contents must be completely new (68). The problem here arises at the moment of recruiting actors: it must be ensured that all of them come from a proletarian background. However, as this was extremely difficult to obtain, given the various class affiliations of workers in a society in transition, part of Keržencev's evaluation contemplates the need to form the new generations (140). Therefore, one of the main preoccupations in the Russia of the times was children's theater for children. Keržencev thinks that there must be no fear that either the bourgeois professional actor or the non-proletarian aficionado poses a threat to the existence of a proletarian theater among workers. On the contrary, he is confident that the working-class environment will end up assimilating both of these characters and put them at the service of the proletariat (70).

Predictably, this question was not sufficiently debated by Latin American praxitioners when they proposed a popular theater, given the perceived ambiguity of Romain Rolland's proposal of a theater *by* the people *for* the people and the class composition of that people. Praxitioners assumed that class-consciousness was easily malleable, adaptable and representable, and that the contact with workers organizations was going to produce a new theater. They were moved by a faith, a political *religion* (as much valid as it was questionable in terms of faith) but the learning process was far from easy in post-colonialist terms. The methodology of collective creation in Latin America would greatly benefit from gathering more information on the class conformation of the groups (at least the most famous ones). As the literature seems to indicate, apart from the casual working-class participant, most group members came from the middle class and with an intellectual formation. It is also necessary to assess the degree of familiarization and cohabitation of such groups with workers sectors. Quite a different case is that of Teatro Escambray and other groups whose task was more involved with peasant groups than with urban workers. Or the case of Teatro de Los Andes, which though it recruited some working-class actors, was not interested in conducting a collectivization of the work of actors. Collective creation, on the other hand, seems to develop and transform very rapidly, as attested by the texts, manifests and all the published material in journals like *Conjunto*, an undisputable leader of theatrical work in Latin America for many years. We would need to establish periods, define stages through the identification of discursive readjustments, the appearance and disappearance of terms, notions and concepts, changes of leadership, work procedures, etc. The constant preoccupation of these groups in justifying their relation with the audience, their insistence on research based on ethnographic incursions into marginalized groups, most of them peasants, leads us to presume that it was a work marked by anxiety (in a psychoanalytical sense), that it experienced a situation of helplessness or isolation they pretended to achieve before an audience —and, even more dangerously, to represent.[58]

Keržencev has detailed the conditions required by any collective work. It is interesting to compare his proposal to the one that later took form in Latin America. Each participant must be able to collaborate in all stages of the creation, analyze the text and his role, represent his character onstage and know the musical part, convey his interpretation of the piece, work in group with the other actors, as well as with all technicians, and the director. The role of director is open to any group member, and the whole group can direct, but at the moment of final staging, this role must be in charge of one person. The text is just a point of departure, the literary aspect of which will be gradual and completely modified by collective re-elaboration. Particular attention must be given not so much to the staging of a particular scene but to the entire spectacle, that is, the creative construction of a new drama play on the basis of a given theme. The spectator may be involved through active participation in the staging work in the form of a critical discussion of what is offered to him, as well as by

[58] The various definitions and etiologies of anguish in the psychoanalytic field (be it in its double Freudian version or the later discussions in the Lacanian and Kleinian fields) could be, undoubtedly, a good guide to begin a political-cultural and ideological theorization on collective creation and the groups that practiced it. It would suffice today to read the texts produced by some groups to measure the degree of fetishization and phobia that, as predictable and calculable elements, seem to indicate such a protection against anguish. Unlike phobia, which appears as fear of an object, in *Seminar 4* Lacan defines anguish as "correlative to the moment of suspension in the subject, at a time in which he does not know where he is, a time in which he is going to turn into something he will never be able to recognize himself in." (228) If anguish, according to Lacan's *Seminar 8*, is a sign that warns the herd of the danger, it is evident that it may come not from the subject himself but from the other, and, in that sense, unlike the animal herd, "the enemy is within himself" (408). And he adds: "What is true on the individual plane, that internal danger, is true also on the plane of the collective. Danger within the subject is the same as danger within the herd." (409) What kind of object were collective creation groups for the Other's desire? What *jouissance* nested in the body of these groups, oppressing them and self-destructing them? Lacan dedicated the entire *Seminar 10* to anguish, in which he introduces the famous object *a*. We shall not go in detail over this, but suffice it to say that the word 'herd' finds echoes in the Nietzschean texts and vocabulary.

participation in mass scenes (90-91). According to Keržencev, these conditions do not ensure that a proletarian theater will be achieved, but neither must we discard the possibility that a proletarian spectacle responding to the new era may arise from individual creation (91).

This methodology can be applied to work on any genre, like opera, tragedy or satire, and its fundamental purpose is to propitiate a new form of action and theatrical representation (92) that appeals to the spectator's participation by introducing, for example, cinematographic images or the old procedure of reading an introduction before the action, or even distributing a playbill in which the argument is presented extensively and in detail. The idea is to present texts that provoke the spectator into participation (92). Keržencev gives much importance to the preparation of spectators for the spectacle, without which, he says, a theatrical revolution is impossible (94). In contrast to our Latin American praxitioners, Keržencev thinks that such a revolution is the result not of any technical method but rather of a complete transformation of the fundamentals of theater (96). Thus, it remains to be assessed to what extent many of the Latin American experiences with collective creation managed to escape the trappings of the imaginary registry—to use Lacan's terms—fascinated as they were by the political content of their proposals but failing to question the politics of gaze—the symbolic registry of theater—imposed by bourgeois theatrical tradition, especially with its Italian-style format (not necessarily contained in a building but easily transported to alternative places, including public squares in street theater).

As for improvisation, Keržencev does not favor an experience of total freedom for the interpreter, but rather a guided improvisation, controlled by the group member who has assumed the direction and knows where unity lies as well as the spectacle's rhythm (99).

The relations of peasant theater with proletarian theater are very complex ones. Keržencev maintains that proletarian theater must prevail over peasant theater (120). The peasantry—in Russia as in Cuba—resists the Revolution insofar as it preserves the influence of a bourgeois and petit-bourgeois past (123). The expressions "workers theater" and "peasant theater" seem to Keržencev rather imprecise, for theater is a manifestation of culture and it would lead us to think that there is a workers' culture as well as a peasant culture. The point here is the substitution of bourgeois culture by a proletarian culture. In this sense, the expression "peasant theater" is so general and vague as the concept of an agricultural world. From the cultural point of view, Keržencev emphasizes, peasant theater will always be the typical theater of the petit bourgeoisie, whose fundamental rule is spontaneity (120-1).

Keržencev is not unaware of the relations between theater and cinema. The success of cinema has been determined by the masses. Thanks to its technical particularity, its relatively low cost, its great transportability, and the extraordinary variety of its repertoire, cinema has impregnated every corner of the nation, including the smallest village and the remotest places. This happens to be the most aged chapter of Keržencev's book, for he followed the development of cinema up to 1923 and criticized the banality or primitiveness of its topics and its usual disregard for the life of the large masses (133). But the fact is that cinema has adapted very well to the task of translating the technical grandiosity of the actions of the masses into artistic images, as well as the strong psychological contrasts inherent in people's nature, especially in those cases in which it reproduces the great epic of social conflicts.

Even more interesting is Keržencev's affirmation, in the chapter dedicated to "Theater and School", of the importance of educating proletarian children in the new artistic sensibility of the new society. Raised in the socialist revolution this new generation, which has not drunk from the capitalist venom, is the best-endowed one to develop the socialist theater so much dreamed of (140). Keržencev believes that children must be involved in school celebrations according to the methods of collective creation, because in this way they will progressively define the meaning of theater, no longer through the bourgeois evocation of the theater hall, the stage and the box, but through theatrical practice itself, from which they will gradually learn to achieve their expression in the field of art and through art. Here Keržencev has an intuition not sufficiently developed amongst Latin American praxitioners: the theatricality of social life. He is not so much preoccupied with the theatricality of theater as with the learning by children of social theatricality. Keržencev perceives the social as a representation: the territory of theater, he says, is very wide. Many aspects of life are impregnated by theatrical elements, and theater occupies many spaces of our life, more than can be reckoned at first sight (141). When planning the theatricality of the social, improvisation and collective creation—the bases of the new proletarian spectacle (189), the popular method of theatrical training (190)—take on a cultural dimension that is not found in our Latin American experience. In fact, Latin American praxitioners and theater people were more obsessed with the relations of collective creation and theater with a supposed 'reality' (always ill-defined or defined very naively) as something lying outside of language. Bourgeois theater is precisely the kind of theater that poses the scene as a representation of reality (hence the discussions on the exactness of such representation, especially in realism-naturalism) conceived of as something outside any kind of semiosis. And it is this bourgeois theater as representation that Keržencev perceives as a museum (154), an historical relic (156), an expositive space for the exhibition of an event that, whatever its ideological commitment, turns the spectator into a passive subject in an attitude of contemplation and distancing.

The new theater, on the other hand, conceived of as a particular theatricalization of social theatricality in general—beginning with *agit prop*, but not limited to it (193)—inspires an ardent enthusiasm, not so much because it collectively stages a grandiose, heroic, revolutionary action as collective experience but because, having left behind opera and ballet, it creates a tragedy in which the main character is the masses (167). Though at some juncture he points at the importance of satire (194) in this transitional process, it is interesting that Keržencev postulates tragedy as a fundamental genre, something that was never present in the horizon of Latin American praxitioners. The consequences of this are countless, but they remain outside the reaches of this essay.

Bibliography

Buenaventura, Enrique. "La elaboración de los Sueños y la Improvisación Teatral". En Buenaventura, Enrique y Jacqueline Vidal. *Esquema General del Método de Trabajo Colectivo del Teatro Experimental de Cali y otros ensayos.* Maracaibo: Universidad de Zulia, 2005. 55-65.

Geirola, Gustavo. *Teatralidad y experiencia política en América Latina.* 1ra. Ed. Irvine, California: Gestos, 2000. 2da. Ed. Buenos Aires/Los Ángeles: Argus-a Artes y Humanidades/Arts & Humanities, 2018.

---. "Ensayando la lógica o la lógica del ensayo: construcción de personaje y temporalidad de la certeza subjetiva". *Teatro XXI* 12.23 (2006): 35-48.

---. *Arte y oficio del director teatral en América Latina: Argentina, Chile, Paraguay y Uruguay.* Buenos Aires: Nueva Generación, 2007a.

---. "Argentina en Cádiz: El psicoanálisis, la nueva dramaturgia y las poéticas actorales". En Beatriz Rizk y Luis Ramos-García, eds. *Panorama de las artes escénicas ibérico y latinoamericanas: Homenaje al Festival Iberoamericano de Cádiz.* Minneapolis-Cádiz: University of Minnesota and Patronato de FIT de Cádiz, 2007b. 55-82.

---. "Aproximación psicoanalítica al ensayo teatral: notas preliminares al concepto de transferencia y el deseo del director". *Aithesis, Revista Chilena de Estudios Estéticos* 46 (2009): 252-269.

Keržencev, Platon Michailovic. *Il Teatro Creativo. Teatro proletario negli anni '20 in Rusia*, con traducción e introducción de Fabrizio Cruziani. Roma: Bulzoni Editore, 1979.

Leach, Robert. *Revolutionary Theatre.* London and New York: Routledge, 1994.

Rolland, Romain. *The People's Theater.* New York: Henry Holt and Co., 1918.

Rudnitsky, Konstantin. *Russian and Soviet Theatre. Tradition and Avant-Garde.* New York: Thames & Hudson, 1998.

For this essay, I worked on the Italian version of Keržencev's book by Fabrizio Cruciani (*Il Teatro Creativo. Teatro proletario negli anni '20 in Russia*), with a translator's introduction. As far as I've been able to establish, this and a German version are the only translations of this work. The only copy available within the California library system is located at the University of California Los Angeles (UCLA). Since my translations are not literal, I have omitted quotation marks but I do refer to the corresponding pages.

Otras publicaciones de Erosbooks:

Gustavo Geirola
Dedicatoria
Sonetos y antisonetos

Gerardo González
Soave Libertate

Otras publicaciones de Argus-*a*:

Gustavo Geirola
Introducción a la praxis teatral.
Creatividad y psicoanálisis

María Cristina Ares
Evita mirada
Modos de ver a Eva Perón:
las figuraciones literarias y visuales de su cuerpo
entre 1992 y 2019

Gustavo Geirola
Los discursos lacanianos y las dramaturgias

Eduardo R. Scarano (compilador)
Racionalidad política de las ciencias y de la tecnología.
Ensayos en homenaje a Ricardo J. Gómez

Virgen Gutiérrez
Con voz de mujer. Entrevistas

Alicia Montes y María Cristina Ares, compiladoras
Régimen escópico y experiencia.
Figuraciones de la mirada y el cuerpo
en la literatura y las artes

Adriana Libonatti y Alicia Serna
De la calle al mundo
Recorridos, imágenes y sentidos en Fuerza Bruta

Laura López Fernández y Luis Mora-Ballesteros (Coords.)
Transgresiones en las letras iberoamericanas:
visiones del lenguaje poético

María Natacha Koss
Mitos y territorios teatrales

Mary Anne Junqueira
A toda vela
El viaje científico de los Estados Unidos:
U.S. Exploring Expedition (1838-1842)

Lyu Xiaoxiao
La fraseología de la alimentación y gastronomía en español.
Léxico y contenido metafórico

Gustavo Geirola
Grotowski soy yo.
Una lectura para la praxis teatral en tiempos de catástrofe

Alicia Montes y María Cristina Ares, comps.
Cuerpo y violencia. De la inermidad a la heterotopía

Gustavo Geirola, comp.
Elocuencia del cuerpo.
Ensayos en homenaje a Isabel Sarli

Lola Proaño Gómez
Poética, Política y Ruptura.
La Revolución Argentina (1966-73): experimento frustrado
De imposición liberal y "normalización" de la economía

Marcelo Donato
El telón de Picasso

Víctor Díaz Esteves y Rodolfo Hlousek Astudillo
Semblanzas y discursos de agrupaciones culturales con bases territoriales en La Araucanía

Sandra Gasparini
Las horas nocturnas. Diez lecturas sobre terror, fantástico y ciencia

Mario A. Rojas, editor
Joaquín Murrieta de Brígido Caro. Un drama inédito del legendario bandido

Alicia Poderti
Casiopea. Vivir en las redes. Ingeniería lingüística y ciber-espacio

Gustavo Geirola
Sueño Improvisación. Teatro. Ensayos sobre la praxis teatral

Jorge Rosas Godoy y Edith Cerda Osses
Condición posthistórica o Manifestación poliexpresiva. Una perturbación sensible

Alicia Montes y María Cristina Ares
Política y estética de los cuerpos. Distribución de lo sensible en la literatura y las artes visuales

Karina Mauro (Compiladora)
Artes y producción de conocimiento. Experiencias de integración de las artes en la universidad

Jorge Poveda
La parergonalidad en el teatro. Deconstrucción del arte de la escena como coeficiente de sus múltiples encuadramientos

Gustavo Geirola
El espacio regional del mundo de Hugo Foguet

Domingo Adame y Nicolás Núñez
Transteatro: Entre, a través y más allá del Teatro

Yaima Redonet Sánchez
Un día en el solar, expresión de la cubanidad de Alberto Alonso

Gustavo Geirola
Dramaturgia de frontera/Dramaturgias del crimen.
A propósito de los teatristas del norte de México

Virgen Gutiérrez
Mujeres de entre mares. Entrevistas

Ileana Baeza Lope
Sara García: ícono cinematográfico nacional mexicano, abuela y lesbiana

Gustavo Geirola
Teatralidad y experiencia política en América Latina (1957-1977)

Domingo Adame
Más allá de la gesticulación
Ensayos sobre teatro y cultura en México

Alicia Montes y María Cristina Ares (compiladoras)
Cuerpos presentes.
Figuracones de la muerte, la enfermedad, la anomalía y el sacrificio.

Lola Proaño Gómez y Lorena Verzero / Compiladoras y editoras
Perspectivas políticas de la escena latinoamericana. Diálogos en tiempo presente

Gustavo Geirola
Praxis teatral. Saberes y enseñanza. Reflexiones a partir del teatro argentino reciente

Alicia Montes
De los cuerpos travestis a los cuerpos zombis. La carne como figura de la historia

Lola Proaño - Gustavo Geirola
¡Todo a Pulmón! Entrevistas a diez teatristas argentinos

Germán Pitta Bonilla
La nación y sus narrativas corporales. Fluctuaciones del cuerpo femenino en la novela sentimental uruguaya del siglo XIX (1880-1907)

Robert Simon
To A Nação, with Love: The Politics of Language through Angolan Poetry

Jorge Rosas Godoy
Poliexpresión o la des-integración de las formas en/desde
La nueva novela *de Juan Luis Martínez*

María Elena Elmiger
DUELO: Íntimo. Privado. Público

María Fernández-Lamarque
Espacios posmodernos en la literature latinoamericana contemporánea: Distopías y heterotopíaa

Gabriela Abad
Escena y escenarios en la transferencia

Carlos María Alsina
De Stanislavski a Brecht: las acciones físicas. Teoría y práctica de procedimientos actorales de construcción teatral

Áqis Núcleo de Pesquisas Sobre Processos de Criação Artística Florianópolis
Falas sobre o coletivo. Entrevistas sobre teatro de grupo

Áqis Núcleo de Pesquisas Sobre Processos de Criação Artística Florianópolis
Teatro e experiências do real (Quatro Estudos)

Gustavo Geirola
El oriente deseado. Aproximación lacaniana a Rubén Darío.

Gustavo Geirola
Arte y oficio del director teatral en América Latina
Tomo I: México y Perú

Gustavo Geirola

Arte y oficio del director teatral en América Latina
Tomo II: Argentina, Chile, Paraguay y Uruguay

Gustavo Geirola

Arte y oficio del director teatral en América Latina
Tomo III: Colombia y Venezuela

Gustavo Geirola

Arte y oficio del director teatral en América Latina
Tomo IV: Bolivia, Brasil y Ecuador

Gustavo Geirola

Arte y oficio del director teatral en América Latina
Tomo V: Centroamérica y Estados Unidos

Gustavo Geirola

Arte y oficio del director teatral en América Latina
Tomo VI: Cuba, Puerto Rico y República Dominicana

Gustavo Geirola

Ensayo teatral, actuación y puesta en escena.
Notas introductorias sobre psicoanálisis y praxis teatral

Argus-*a*
Artes y Humanidades / Arts and Humanities
Los Ángeles – Buenos Aires
2023

Made in the USA
Monee, IL
05 November 2026

67807953R00072